Mollie MAKES

PATCHWORK

CHARMING QUILTED PROJECTS
PLUS TIPS & TRICKS

{Contents

INTRODUCTION 4

Get piecing!

When I think patchwork, I think of my auntie. Her craft room is a thing to behold— all color-coordinating baskets of rainbow fabrics, buttons, beads, and threads. She makes such beautiful quilted bags and cushions, and whenever I visit she still lets me choose one to keep.

The texture, intricacy, and effort that goes into this work are all so appealing to the senses. Choosing your fabrics is a complete joy, and the pride you feel when your work is complete? So, so good!

Whatever your level of skill with this time-honored craft, we have it covered here. With techniques and plenty of beautiful modern projects to try, it's all you need to get started and embark on your own stitching journey.

Lara

Lara Watson
Editor, *Mollie Makes*

Note
Measurements are given in imperial and metric: choose one or the other and stick to it for each project or technique—do not be tempted to mix and match.

Projects

Brick pattern curtain

This unlined curtain panel is a perfect way to hide the clutter on open shelving and it is hung by threading a curtain rod through the channel at the top. It is a great project for using up your favorite fabric scraps and the brick pattern piecing will look just as good in solids as it does in prints.

MATERIALS

One piece of gingham cotton fabric 32⅛ x 8⅝" (82 x 22 cm) for top panel

21 pieces of cotton fabric each 8⅝ x 5½" (22 x 14 cm) for the full bricks

Six pieces of cotton fabric each 4¾ x 5½" (12 x 14 cm) for the half bricks

Sticky notes

White sewing thread

Pinking shears (optional)

Curtain rod for hanging

SIZE

34½ x 30¼" (88 x 77 cm)

FEATURED TECHNIQUES

- Making templates (page 90)
- Machine piecing (page 98)
- For more on brick piecing and variations, see page 106

BEFORE YOU BEGIN

The curtain was made with a finished size to hang from a kitchen worktop to hide a standard-size appliance, and you may need to adjust the size to fit your appliance. To make a pair of curtains to hang in a window, line the back with a plain fabric.

Prewash and press fabrics before use as necessary: this is particularly important if you are using vintage fabrics as these may have dyes that run when washed.

To cut out your fabrics, you can make a full brick template measuring 8⅝ x 5½" (22 x 14 cm) and a half brick template measuring 4¾ x 5½" (12 x 14 cm) from template plastic. (These template sizes include seam allowances.)

When piecing the patchwork, pin and stitch together with right sides facing. **All seams are ⅜" (1 cm) unless otherwise stated.**

Patchwork Story

One day when I was folding up some fabrics to store away, I noticed how sweet they looked together and thought I'd like to make them into a patchwork. It had to be a quick project that wouldn't use much fabric, so I made this little curtain to hang in the kitchen. It covers up our washing machine and is so bright and cheerful that it makes doing the laundry a much happier job.

METHOD

{01} Lay out your fabric pieces
Following the patchwork piecing diagram, lay out your fabric pieces, arranging them so that no two pieces of the same fabric are next to each other: start with a row of solid brick pieces; the second row will be offset, so start and end this row with a half brick piece. Continue the rows to complete the brick pattern layout. It is a good idea to take a quick photograph of your fabric layout at this stage for future reference if needed. Place a sticky note on the first (left-hand) piece of each horizontal row and number 1 to 6. Gather up the first row in order so that the numbered fabric piece is on top, and pin together. Gather up each row in turn to give you six piles of fabric.

{02} Piece the brick pattern panel
Begin sewing the first row of fabric pieces together, then continue to sew the pieces in each row in turn to give you six horizontal rows, pressing all seams to one side as you go. Sew each row together in order (use your number stickers to remind you, then remove).

{03} Add the top panel to the patchwork panel
Align the top panel to the top edge of the patchwork panel with right sides facing and stitch together. Press the seam open.

{04} Finish the curtain
To hem the sides and bottom of the curtain, fold over the edges twice, then press and stitch 6 mm (¼") from the edge. To hem the top and make a channel for the curtain rod, fold over 1⅛" (3 cm), then fold over another 1⅛" (3 cm); pin, then stitch, leaving each end open. (The channel depth can be adjusted to fit the overall length required, but do check that you can thread the curtain wire through it.)

As the reverse of this curtain will not be visible, it is unlined, but, to prevent fraying, it is a good idea to finish the seams with pinking shears. Press the panel, thread the curtain rod through the channel, and hang.

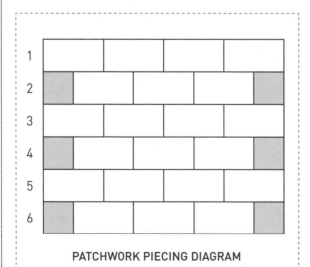

PATCHWORK PIECING DIAGRAM

Note
To line the curtain panel, work to the end of step 3, then measure the panel and cut out a piece of lining fabric to the same size. Pin lining and curtain right sides together. Sew along the sides and bottom, leaving the top edge open. Turn right side out and press. Hem the top edge as described in step 4, leaving the ends open to thread the curtain wire through.

JANE HUGHES

Jane from littleteawagon is a crafter/designer with a fondness for fabrics and sewing, doodling and making and blogging about a crafty life.
www.teawagontales.blogspot.com

Nine-patch beanbag

{ *This super-comfy beanbag is pieced using simple squares with a nine-patch top. It's a great way to explore combining vintage fabrics with contemporary prints. A few scuttling beetles have been appliquéd over the finished patches, which are a great way for beginners to hide less than perfect pieced seams!*

MATERIALS

Four pieces of fabric each 24 x 24"
(60 x 60 cm) for pieced top and sides

One piece of cord or hard-wearing fabric
20 x 20" (50 x 50 cm) for base panel

One piece of stiff iron-on interfacing
39 x 53" (100 x 135 cm)

Black felt 16 x 8" (40 x 20 cm)
for appliqué

Zipper 18" (45 cm)

Beanbag liner

About 3 cubic feet (1 cubic meter)
polystyrene beans

Embroidery floss: black and green

Sewing threads to match fabrics

SIZE

20 x 20 x 12" (50 x 50 x 30 cm)

FEATURED TECHNIQUES

- Making templates (page 90)
- Machine piecing (page 98)
- Appliqué techniques (page 136)
- Basic hand stitches (page 95)
- For more on nine-patch piecing and
  variations, see page 112

BEFORE YOU BEGIN

Prewash and press fabrics before use as
necessary: this is particularly important
if you are using vintage fabrics as these
may have dyes that run when washed.

Make a 6¾" (17 cm) square template
from template plastic. (This template
size includes seam allowances.)

When piecing the patchwork, pin and
sew your fabrics together with right
sides facing. **Seam allowances are
3⁄8" (1 cm) throughout.**

Patchwork Story

I created my very first nine-patch beanbag for my cat Moy, and she absolutely loves it. It was one of the first patchwork projects I ever made and I loved its simplicity. I really enjoy how patchwork lets you mix different fabrics together, recycling old and new. I love learning new techniques and creating colorful, unique pieces of work. You could swap my beetle appliqués with your own designs to make the beanbag personal to you.

METHOD

{01} Cut and lay out your fabrics

Using your square plastic template, cut out a total of 33 squares from your four chosen fabrics: we used eight squares of beige cord, calico, and green patterned fabric, and nine squares of vintage purple fabric.

Following the patchwork piecing diagram, lay out your squares, arranging them so that no two squares of the same fabric are next to each other: nine squares are required for the top panel, with six squares making up each side panel.

{02} Piece the top and side panels

Starting with the top panel (the nine-patch unit), take the first row

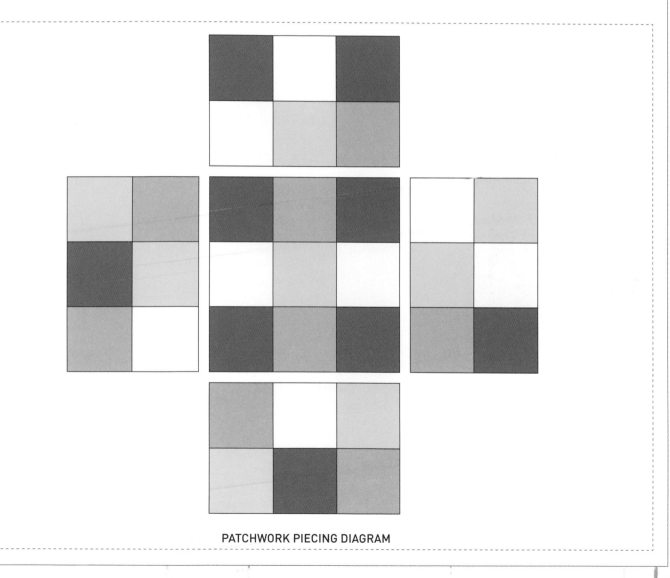

PATCHWORK PIECING DIAGRAM

of three squares, pin together, then sew. Repeat to piece row 2 and row 3. Press seams open.

Pin together the pieced rows 1 and 2 taking care to align seams, and stitch. Repeat to join row 3. Your top panel is now complete.

Piece each side panel in the same way, first joining three squares to give you two rows, then joining the rows to give you a six-square panel.

PENNY FORBES

Penny Forbes has been a maker for as long as she can remember. For inspiration she collects curiosities and she loves quirky and unusual things. Sugar skulls are a favorite theme for much of her work and she loves using bright colors and recycling old materials to make new things. You can find her on Facebook under her business name, pegeggleg.

{03} Back panels and insert zipper

To ensure the beanbag maintains its shape, each of the pieced panels are backed with a stiff iron-on interfacing. Cut five pieces of the interfacing to size to match the pieced top and side panels and use to back the fabric pieces following the manufacturer's instructions.

Now insert the zipper. First, take two fabric off-cuts about 2 x 4" (5 x 10 cm) and fold each piece in half. Stitch the fabric pieces along the folded edge at each end of the zipper (see diagram right). Take one of the side panels and pin the zipper on with right sides facing as in the diagram below. Stitch all the way along the unpinned edge. Remove pins and fold open the zipper panel.

{04} Add the appliqué

Using the beetle body templates on page 154 and tailor's chalk, draw and cut out four (or more!) beetles from the black felt. Cut ⅜" (1 cm) wide strips of felt for the legs—you'll need six for each beetle. Pin the beetle

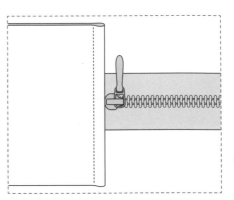

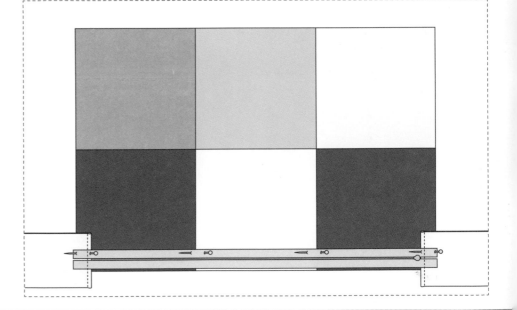

bodies and legs in place and carefully machine stitch around the edge of the body and down each leg. (If you position the legs over the seams where the squares are joined, they can hide any imperfect seams.)

Use black embroidery floss to complete the leg detailing with backstitch. Embroider backstitch antennas onto the heads, and finish the top of each antenna with a French knot. Use green embroidery floss to add a simple embroidered pattern to the shells if you wish.

{05} Assemble the beanbag

Place the base panel on top of the side panel with zipper, right sides facing, aligning the edge of the zipper and edge of the base panel.

Sew along the length of the zipper, then open out the joined panels.

Join together the remaining three side panels to make a strip, working with right sides facing each time. Pin each end of the side-panel strip to each side of the remaining side panel, again with right sides facing, to form a loop (see diagram). Stitch together.

Pin the unjoined side panels to the remaining three sides of the base panel, carefully lining up the seams, and stitch together. Unzip the beanbag before pinning and sewing the top panel onto the side panels, working with right sides facing. Turn the assembled beanbag right way out through the zipper opening. Insert the beanbag liner and fill with beans. Take a seat!

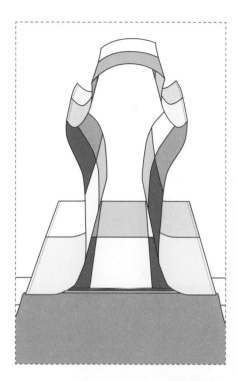

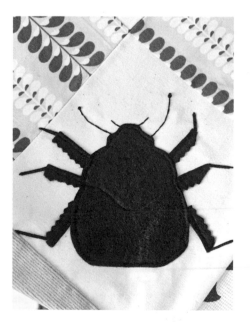

Giant rainbow star quilt

{ This bold double-bed size quilt, made from bright rainbow colors and large-scale vintage prints, is a fun take on a traditional quilt block design—the eight-pointed star. Filled with lofty batting, it's more of a comforter or coverlet than a quilt. The quilt layers are tied together, rather than being machine quilted and bound, so it makes an ideal project for a beginner.

MATERIALS

Eight pieces of printed cotton fabric each at least 21¼ x 21¼" (54 x 54 cm) for the triangle squares in the following colors: dark pink, light pink, dark navy, light navy, dark green, light green, dark orange, light orange

Eight pieces of printed cotton fabric each at least 20½ x 20½" (52 x 52 cm) for the full squares in the following colors: dark red, light red, dark purple, light purple, dark turquoise, light turquoise, dark yellow, light yellow

One cotton double-bed flat sheet minimum size 79½ x 79½" (202 x 202 cm) for backing

One piece of thick (high-loft) polyester batting 78¾ x 78¾" (200 x 200 cm)

White sewing thread

Red cotton perlé embroidery floss

Temporary basting spray

SIZE

78¾ x 78¾" (200 x 200 cm)

FEATURED TECHNIQUES

- Machine piecing (page 98)
- Simple tied quilting (page 148)
- Basic hand stitches (page 95)
- Making a quilt sandwich (page 146)

BEFORE YOU BEGIN

Prewash and press fabrics before use as necessary: this is particularly important if you are using vintage fabrics as these may have dyes that run when washed.

When piecing the patchwork, pin and stitch together with right sides facing. **All seam allowances are ⅜" (1 cm) throughout.** Use of a walking foot (see page 88) is recommended.

METHOD

{01} Cut your fabrics

For the square pieces:
Cut 20½" (52 cm) squares from dark red, light red, dark yellow, light yellow, dark turquoise, light turquoise, dark purple, and light purple fabrics (eight pieces in all).

For the triangle pieces:
Cut 21¼" (54 cm) squares from dark orange, light orange, dark pink, light pink, dark green, light green, dark navy and light navy fabrics. Cut each diagonally to make two triangles (16 pieces in all)—see fig A.

If necessary cut your backing sheet to 79½ x 79½" (202 x 202 cm).

{02} Piece the top panel

Note: After sewing, all seams need to be pressed away from the lightest fabric.

Join the triangles together (dark green to light green, dark orange to light orange, etc) to form square blocks by matching the longest sides of the triangles. Press and trim excess fabric from seam corners. This will give you eight 20½" (52 cm) triangle squares.

Join matching triangle squares together with light fabrics in the center to form a larger triangle (see fig B) to give you four side panels.

Join the four dark fabric squares, taking care to match the seams in the center—see fig C.

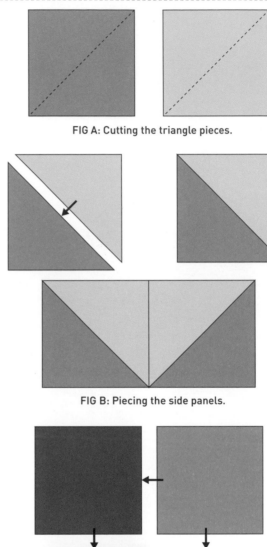

FIG A: Cutting the triangle pieces.

FIG B: Piecing the side panels.

FIG C: Piecing the center panel.

Join the remaining light fabric squares to the navy and orange side panels as shown in fig D, then join each pieced side to the pieced center panel, taking care to match corners. Trim edges if required.

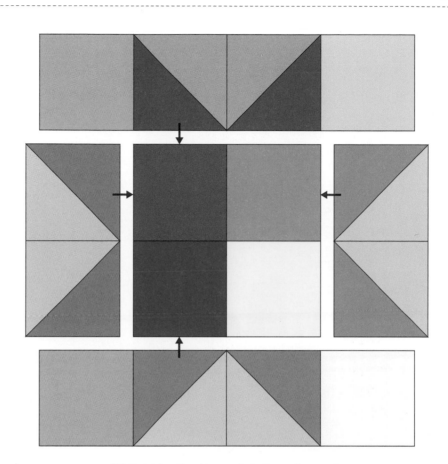

FIG D: Joining the side panels to the center panel.

CINTIA GONZALEZ
AKA MY POPPET

Cintia is a maker and craft blogger. She loves collecting and using vintage fabrics, re-purposing unwanted textiles and garments, and generally creating something useful and beautiful out of things that were previously unloved. Rather than buying new, most of her sewing supplies are gleaned from thrift stores or flea markets. To find out more, visit her at mypoppet.com.au.

Patchwork Story

The large scale of this quilt allows the big, graphic vintage prints to be shown off to their full potential. As a collector of vintage, I'm always looking for fun and practical ways to use my colorful collection without having to cut my fabric up into small pieces. I liked the idea of tying this quilt, as machine or hand quilting such a large quilt takes skill and a lot of patience, and the little red thread tufts add a textural element to the patchwork.

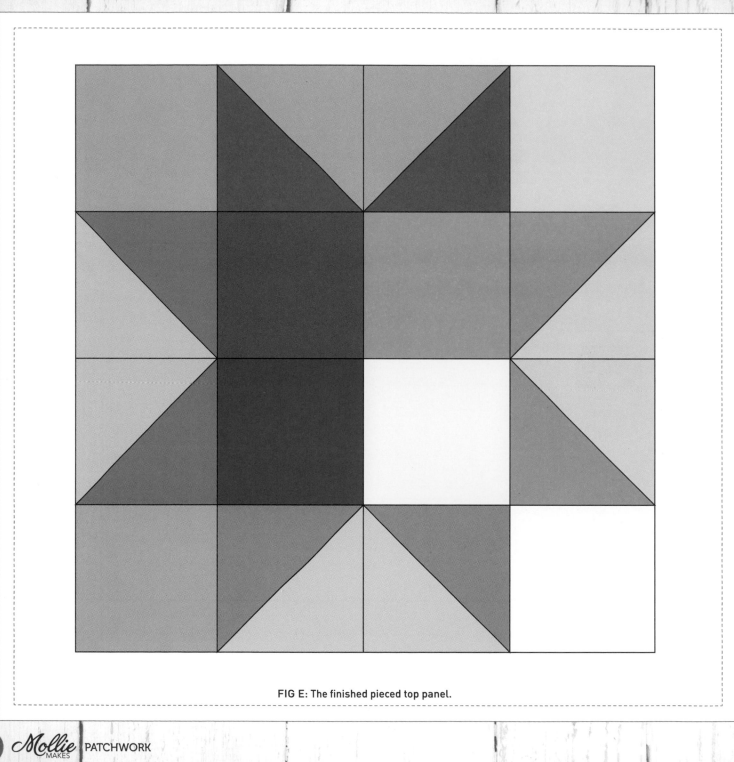

FIG E: The finished pieced top panel.

{03} Assemble the quilt

Spray glue the batting to fix it to the wrong side of the quilt backing (see page 147), keeping the outer seam allowance clear. Lay the patchwork top panel right side facing up on the floor and lay the backing sheet right side facing down on top, lining up the edges. Pin to secure. Sew all the way around the outside edge leaving an opening of about 24" (60 cm). Turn the quilt right side out and hand stitch the opening closed using whipstitch.

{04} Work the tied quilting

Using a double thickness of embroidery floss and following fig F, sew ties through the layers on the center and corner of each square, and halfway down each diagonal seam, with the knots worked in a grid pattern about 9¾" (25 cm) apart (see page 148).

Once the tied quilting is complete, remove the pins and fluff up the batting for a lofty eiderdown effect.

For the tied quilting, work ⅜" (1 cm) long stitches and trim thread to leave a ⅜" (1 cm) tail like a little tassel.

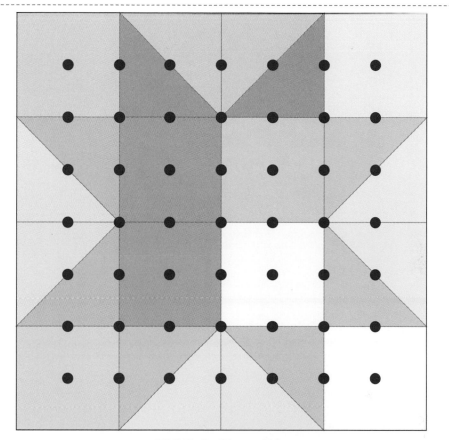

FIG F: Tied quilting positions.

Rail fence owl hanging

Fancy a bit of strip piecing? This little hanging is a great way to get started. A cute yet quirky owl swoops across a patchwork background pieced using four different fabrics. We've gone for calm corals and a bit of mustard to suggest the sunlit canopy of the woods, but don't be afraid to go wild with your colors if you want a bolder piece.

MATERIALS

Four fat quarters of contrasting cotton fabric

One piece of cotton fabric 34 x 18" (86 x 46 cm) for the backing

Four strips of 1½" (4 cm) wide cotton fabric: two 30" (76 cm) each for top and bottom binding and two 18" (46 cm) each for side bindings

One piece of calico 23 x 10" (58.5 x 25 cm) for the owl appliqué

One piece of medium-weight batting or interfacing 32 x 20" (81 x 50 cm)

Three pieces of ribbon 6" (15 cm) long for hanging loops

Wooden pole 32" (80 cm) long for hanging (optional)

Cream sewing thread

Brown embroidery floss

Sticky notes

Mini grid maker (optional)

SIZE

28 x 16" (71 x 40.5 cm)

FEATURED TECHNIQUES

- Rotary cutting (page 92)
- Machine piecing (page 98)
- Cut-and-sew hand appliqué (page 136)
- Basic hand stitches (page 95)
- Making a quilt sandwich (page 146)
- Machine quilting: In-the-ditch (page 149)
- Single binding (page 151)
- For more on rail fence piecing and variations, see page 104

BEFORE YOU BEGIN

Prewash and press your fabrics before use as necessary: this is particularly important if you are using vintage fabrics as these may have dyes that run when washed. If you are not using fat quarters, you'll need fabric pieces about 18 x 22" (46 x 55 cm).

For clean accurate cutting measurements, use a rotary cutter, quilter's rule (or mini grid maker) and cutting mat to cut out your strips for piecing.

When piecing the patchwork, pin and stitch together with right sides facing. **All seams are ¼" (6 mm) unless otherwise stated.**

The project mixes hand and machine sewing, but it can easily be done all by hand if you prefer, although it will take a good deal longer.

METHOD

{01} Cut and piece your fabric strips

From each of the four contrasting fabrics cut seven strips each measuring 22 x 1½" (56 x 4 cm). Sort your fabric strips into seven piles each containing the four fabrics in the same order. Take each bundle and sew each of the four strips together, checking as you go that the strips are all facing the correct way and are being sewn together in the same order. Once stitching is complete, press the seams to one side.

{02} Cut the joined fabric strips into squares

Use a ruler (or mini grid maker) to cut each of the seven joined fabric strips into squares measuring exactly 4½ x 4½" (11.5 x 11.5 cm). Each strip should give you four squares (28 squares in total).

{03} Lay out the rail fence patchwork

Following the patchwork piecing diagram, lay out your rail fence pattern in rows of seven squares across and four down, alternating the squares horizontally and vertically. Double check that the squares are placed so that the strips run in the same order, to ensure that the four-fabric rail fence pattern is formed.

Place a sticky note on the first (left-hand) piece of each horizontal row and number 1 to 4. Gather

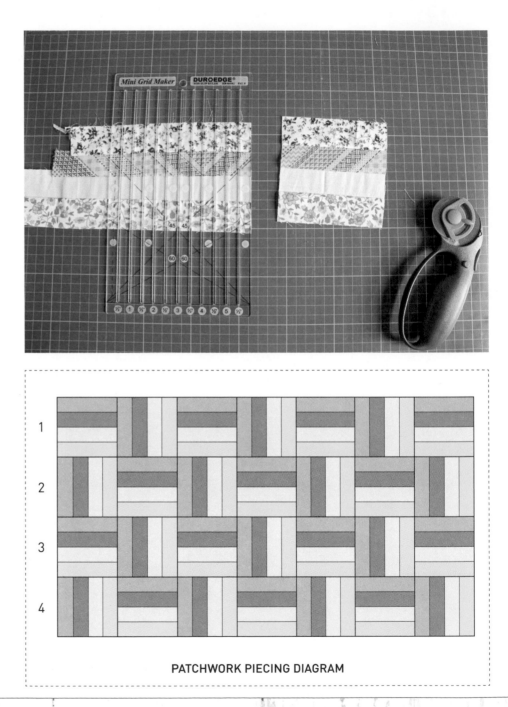

PATCHWORK PIECING DIAGRAM

up the first row in order with the numbered piece on top. Gather up the other rows in turn to give you four stacks of squares.

Now carefully sew together each square in the first row, pinning each square in place as you go. Each joined square should be exactly 4" (10 cm) wide so keep checking this measurement as you work. Press the seams in alternate directions and cut off any loose threads. Stitch together rows 2, 3, and 4 in the same way.

Join the four rows to complete the pieced background. When you are sewing the rows together, line them up by pinning from the center squares out to the edge, as this will help to keep the squares in line. The aim is for seams to match perfectly across the rows. Press the patchwork piece and cut off any loose threads.

{04} Make the appliqué owl
Enlarge the owl template on pages 154–155, carefully joining the pieces with double-sided tape. Cut it out and draw around it to mark the outline of the owl onto the calico. To transfer the embroidery guidelines onto the fabric, tape the template to a window, place the calico over the template, and go over the markings with a very fine pencil or disappearing fabric marker.

Cut out around the outline of the owl and pin it centrally onto the patchwork panel, angling the

Patchwork Story

I love owls—who doesn't? I've had a few falconry lessons and I'm always amazed when they fly up toward you. The shape their wings make is amazing and I've used a simplified version of this to create my silhouette. The rail fence patchwork makes a very effective backdrop and is great for using up any fabric pieces you have spare. I love to use material in my work that has been handed down from friends or relatives as it often has a story or memory attached to it.

The raw edges of the calico will fray to give the impression of feathers.

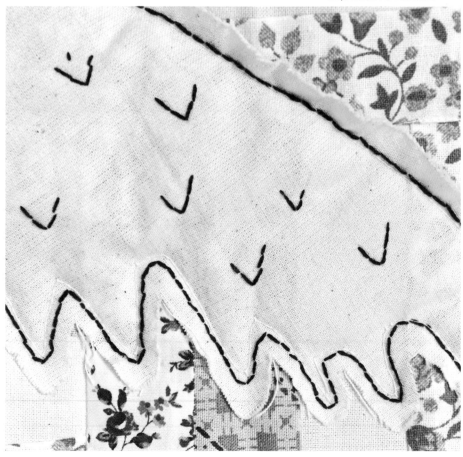

body slightly to give the impression that the owl is swooping through trees. Using the brown embroidery floss and backstich (see page 95), embroider the head first, then the body, and finally the wings from the shoulders out, as this will help to prevent the fabric from puckering. You may need to move the pins to flatten out the owl appliqué as you stitch. Trim any loose threads and press.

{05} Assemble and quilt the panel
Make a quilt sandwich (see page 146) with your backing fabric wrong side up, then the piece of batting or interfacing over the backing fabric, and then the patchwork panel on top with right side facing up. (The batting and the backing fabric should both be larger than the patchwork panel as once the quilting is complete, the layers will be trimmed flush.)

Using the cream sewing thread, machine stitch around the owl to start to join the three layers together. Stitch as close to your brown floss embroidery line as possible, head first, then body and lastly wings, checking as you go that the owl appliqué stays as flat as possible. (It is not necessary to machine stitch

KIRSTY ANDERSON
AKA A WOODEN TREE

Designer-maker Kirsty Anderson creates textile pieces using vintage and sourced fabrics, turning them into unique textile works that take on a new life. Using inspiration from the past, wildlife, family, and eclectic items that hold history, she creates a whole range of animal art, from giant narwhals to Mr Stag textile wall hangings. You can see more of Kirsty's work at www.awoodentree.com.

along the "detail" feathers across the wings and body.)

To complete the quilting, stitch in-the-ditch (see photo opposite), sewing in between the main joins of the patchwork piecing, stitching from the center out to minimize bumps or puckers. Working from the *edge* of the owl (do not stitch over the owl), stitch the vertical lines first, then the horizontal lines.

{06} Add binding and make hanging loops

Trim and neaten the edges around the quilted panel and trim any loose threads. The panel is bound with a single binding (see page 151). The shorter strips are attached first, then the longer strips. To make the hanging loops, fold each of the ribbon lengths in half, then fold the raw edges under ½" (1.3 cm), and,

working on the back of the panel, pin one to each top corner and one to the top center. Machine or hand stitch in place. Thread a wooden dowel through the loops to hang up the finished panel.

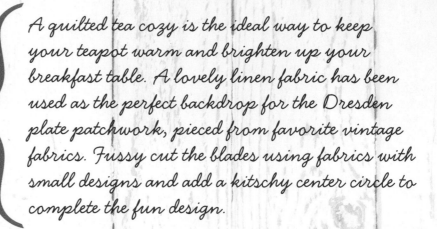

Dresden plate tea cozy

A quilted tea cozy is the ideal way to keep your teapot warm and brighten up your breakfast table. A lovely linen fabric has been used as the perfect backdrop for the Dresden plate patchwork, pieced from favorite vintage fabrics. Fussy cut the blades using fabrics with small designs and add a kitschy center circle to complete the fun design.

MATERIALS

One piece of cotton or cotton/linen fabric ⅓ yard (0.3 meters) for the tea cozy front and back

One piece of cotton fabric ⅓ yard (0.3 meters) for the lining

Two pieces of low-loft cotton batting each 15 x 15" (38 x 38 cm)

20 small scraps of cotton fabric each at least 3 x 3" (7.5 x 7.5 cm) for the blades of the Dresden plate

One piece of cotton fabric with motif 5 x 5" (13 x 13 cm) for the center of the Dresden plate

1 yard (1 meter) of bias binding tape

Narrow ribbon for tab 4" (10 cm)

Sewing thread

Temporary basting spray (optional)

SIZE

12½ x 9" (32 x 23 cm)

FEATURED TECHNIQUES

- Making templates (page 90)
- Machine piecing (page 98)
- Appliqué techniques (page 136)
- Machine quilting (page 149)
- Binding (page 151)
- For more on Dresden plate piecing, see page 133

BEFORE YOU BEGIN

Prewash and press fabrics before use as necessary: this is particularly important if you are using vintage fabrics as these may have dyes that run when washed.

Make templates for the Dresden plate blade and center circle (page 157) from template plastic.

All seams are ¼" (6 mm) unless otherwise stated.

Patchwork Story

As a quilting instructor, I encourage students to find other applications for the techniques they learn in class. For instance, the Dresden plate appliquéd onto separate blocks and pieced together would make a lovely quilt. It's also a great design for dressing up tea towels or the center of a pillow cover. If your project requires a smaller or larger motif, enlarging or reducing the size of the blade on your printer can easily accomplish this.

METHOD

{01} Cut your tea cozy fabrics

Enlarge and trace the tea cozy pattern on page 157 onto paper and cut out. Take your piece of fabric for the tea cozy front and back, and fold it so the selvedges meet in the middle of the piece of fabric (see photo). Pin the tea cozy pattern in place along the left-hand edge of the folded fabric and cut out. Now flip the tea cozy template and pin onto the right-hand edge of the folded fabric to cut a second tea cozy piece. Repeat to cut two tea cozy shapes from your lining fabric.

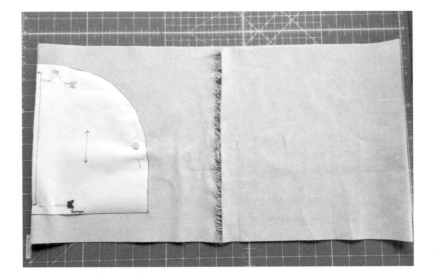

{02} Cut your patchwork fabrics

Use the Dresden plate blade template to mark out and cut 20 blades from your scrap fabrics. The blades are rather small, but can be fussy cut to reveal charming elements (see page 88). Use the Dresden plate center circle to cut an interesting motif for the center of the Dresden plate and set aside.

{03} Prepare the Dresden plate blades

Take the 20 pieces of fabric cut for the Dresden plate blades, fold each in half lengthwise (right sides facing) and stitch across the wide end. It is a good idea to reduce your stitch length when sewing such small pieces. Turn each blade right side out and push out the point, using a chop stick to get a nice sharp point:

the seam should be in the center of the back of the blade point (see diagram below). Press.

Arrange the blades in a circle. With right sides facing, stitch the blades together along the long sides to form the circle. Once complete, press all seam allowances in one direction and set aside. *(Note: The center circle is added later.)*

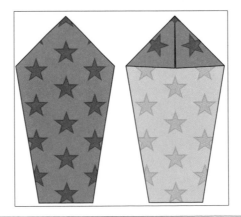

{04} Prepare and quilt tea cozy front and back

Place a batting square on the wrong side of the tea cozy front and back, and secure in place using temporary basting spray or straight pins. Machine quilt with a simple 1" (2.5 cm) grid pattern. Trim the batting even with the edges of the cozy front and back.

Place the Dresden plate circle centrally on the front of the tea cozy and secure in place with temporary basting spray (or pins). Machine quilt around the edges of the blades to secure in place. Take the center circle, turn under the seam allowance and hand stitch to the middle of the Dresden plate using the turned-edge hand appliqué technique (see page 137).

{05} Assemble the tea cozy

To make the tea cozy tab, take the ribbon and fold in half. Place the folded tab to the top edge of the tea cozy front, raw edges aligning, so that the ribbon loop is facing down, and baste in place.

Stack the tea cozy fabric pieces in the following order: front lining right side up, back lining wrong side up, quilted front of cozy right side up, quilted back of cozy wrong side up. Pin the layers together.

Starting at the bottom left-hand edge, machine stitch all the way around the curve of the tea cozy making sure to catch all layers in the stitching. Do not stitch the straight bottom edge closed. Turn the tea cozy right side out and smooth the lining. Trim up the bottom edge if needed. Stitch around the opening with a small zigzag stitch to hold everything in place. Bind the bottom edge with bias tape to finish. Put the kettle on!

MARY DUGAN

Mary began stitching as a child, creating dolls' clothes from her grandmother's scrap fabrics. With more than 25 years' experience of quilting, she teaches her craft at her local quilt shop. She loves traditional quilts with a modern twist, usually hand quilting her creations with a big stitch and cotton perlé. You can see more of her work by visiting her blog at www.mollyflanders.blogspot.com.

Hexagon picnic blanket

For this bold, bright blanket, large fabric hexagons are machine stitched together. The larger scale works really well here, but you could just as easily reduce the size of the hexagons to make a baby quilt or cushion using the traditional English paper piecing method. For an even more functional finish, swap the fleece backing for waterproof oilcloth.

MATERIALS

14 pieces of cotton fabric in a variety of colors and patterns each 22 x 22" (55 x 55 cm) for hexagon patchwork panel

One piece of soft fleece fabric 51 x 54" (128 x 135 cm) for backing

½ yard (0.5 meters) of 44–45" (112 cm) wide cotton fabric for binding

Sewing thread

Sticky notes

SIZE

Approx 54 x 51" (135 x 128 cm)

FEATURED TECHNIQUES

- Making templates (page 90)
- Machine piecing (page 98)
- Machine quilting (page 149)
- Continuous binding (page 152)

DESIGNED BY JANE HUGHES

BEFORE YOU BEGIN

Prewash and press all fabric before use as necessary: this is important if you are using vintage fabrics as these may have dyes that will run when washed.

Make the hexagon paper template following the instructions given on the template (see page 158). The template includes seam allowances.

When piecing the patchwork, pin and stitch together with right sides facing. **All seams are ⅜" (1 cm) unless otherwise stated.**

Patchwork Story

I love patchwork, I love colors, I love going on picnics and I love hexagons, so I had the idea to make a bold, colorful patchwork blanket that would be good to sit on, come rain or shine. Patchwork means different things to different people, but to me it means color, shapes and lots of lovely fabrics!

METHOD

{01} Cut out your fabrics

Using the hexagon template, neatly cut out 28 full hexagons from your chosen fabrics. Referring to the patchwork piecing diagram, you will see that the filler pieces fit into the gaps at the sides and along the top of the full hexagon pieces. You will need 18 filler pieces in all. Use your paper pattern and fold to size to cut the filler pieces from your chosen fabrics as required (use the patchwork piecing diagram to guide you to the shapes required for fit).

{02} Lay out your fabrics

Working on a clean floor, start by laying out the full hexagons. Use the patchwork piecing diagram as your guide, and start with the first full vertical row of hexagons—row 2, which has been shaded on the diagram. Once you have placed all 28 full hexagons, stand back and review: do you have a good balance of colors and patterns? Try to avoid putting similar colors or patterns next to each other. If you are happy with the layout, you can start to fill in the gaps around the edges with the 18 cut-to-fit hexagon pieces.

Once the layout is complete, check you are happy with it, then take a quick photo to refer back to later if necessary. Using your sticky notes, number each row 1 to 7, as in the patchwork piecing diagram. Working from the bottom of each row up, gather up the pieces in a pile and pin the numbered sticky note to the top piece.

(03) Sew together the hexagon pieces in each row

It is really important to note here that accurate sewing is the key to making the points on the hexagons neat and flat. So now is a good time to mark your start and stop sewing points. Using a disappearing marker pen or a pencil, mark an X ⅜" (1 cm) from the edges of each point. Machine stitch the pieces

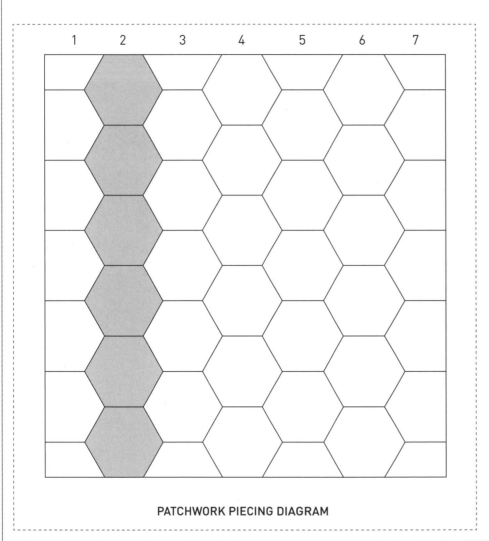

PATCHWORK PIECING DIAGRAM

in each numbered pile together in order, making sure each seam stops exactly at the center of the marked X and backstitching to secure. When you have finished you will have seven rows.

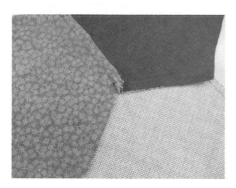

{04} Sew together the rows of pieced hexagons

Starting at the top, sew rows 1 and 2 together. Continue marking the X points before sewing if you wish. Make sure you fold over the hexagon above the one you are sewing to keep it flat and out of the way.

Continue adding the rows using this method until you have completed the patchwork. Press the seams.

{05} Back and bind the blanket

Lay the fleece fabric right side down (if you are able to work on a wooden floor, you can use masking tape to stick it down to keep it flat). Lay the patchwork piece on top right side facing up, and pin all the way around the edges and in the center to keep the layers in place.

Machine stitch together all the way around the edge with a ¼" (5 mm) seam. Trim off any excess fleece to make sure the cut edges are neat and straight.

For the binding, cut strips 2⅜" (6 cm) wide from your backing fabric and join to make a continuous strip about 6 yards (5.5 meters) long. The blanket is bound with a continuous binding. For full instructions, see Making a Quilt: Continuous Binding, page 152).

Broken dishes floor cushion

{ *If you are a sewer, one of life's eternal problems is what to do with all the small leftover bits of material. This large patchwork floor cushion will make a serious dent in your stash pile. The oversized broken dishes block is actually made from four blocks constructed from lots of simple-to-piece triangles and squares.* }

MATERIALS

Large variety of solid and patterned cotton fabric scraps each measuring at least 4 x 4" (10 x 10 cm)

1 yard (1 meter) of 44–45" (112 cm) wide cotton fabric in neutral shade

1 yard (1 meter) of 44–45" (112 cm) wide cotton calico

1 yard (1 meter) of 44–45" (112 cm) wide coordinating cotton fabric for cushion back

¼ yard (0.25 meters) of 44–45" (112 cm) wide coordinating cotton fabric for binding

One piece of cotton batting about 36 x 36" (91 x 91 cm)

Machine sewing thread

Zipper 30" (77 cm)

Cushion pad 30 x 30" (77 x 77 cm)

SIZE

About 30 x 30" (77 x 77 cm)

FEATURED TECHNIQUES

- Triangle squares (page 100)
- Machine piecing (page 98)
- Making a quilt sandwich (page 146)
- Machine quilting (page 149)
- Continuous binding (page 152)
- For more on broken dishes piecing and variations, see page 118

MALKA DUBRAWSKY

Malka has a Bachelor of Fine Arts degree in Studio Art and many years' experience working as a fiber artist. She is the author of two books, designs fabric ranges for Moda Fabrics, and most recently she has been busy making functional textiles using her own hand-dyed and patterned fabric. For all her latest creations, visit her online store www.stitchindye.etsy.com.

BEFORE YOU BEGIN

Use up your fabric scraps: about 45 different print and solid off-cuts were used to create the cushion as shown.

Prewash and press fabrics before use as necessary: this is particularly important if you are using vintage fabrics as these may have dyes that run when washed.

When piecing the patchwork, pin and stitch together with right sides facing. **All seams are ¼" (6 mm) unless otherwise stated.** Unless otherwise directed, press all seams to one side, alternating sides where seams intersect.

The broken dishes floor cushion design is made by combining four blocks, and it is best to piece them one at a time, to ensure that your fabric selection coordinates well in each block. For the layout of the broken dishes floor cushion block, see the photo below and refer often to this as you make up the elements required to make each block.

Layout of block E: four of these blocks are required to make the oversized broken dishes block.

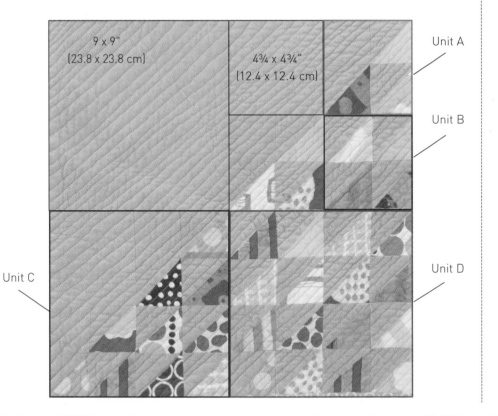

METHOD

{01} Cut your patchwork fabrics
Cut the following pieces:
From selection of prints and solids:
144 squares measuring 3 x 3"
(7.5 x 7.5 cm).

From cotton fabric in neutral shade:
144 squares measuring 3 x 3"
(7.5 x 7.5 cm)
16 squares measuring 2⅝ x 2⅝"
(6.7 x 6.7 cm)
8 squares measuring 4¾ x 4¾"
(12.4 x 12.4 cm)
4 squares measuring 9 x 9"
(23.8 x 23.8 cm)

{02} Make triangle squares
Each of the broken dishes floor cushion blocks requires you to make a total of 36 triangle squares. Working with the 3 x 3" (7.5 x 7.5 cm) fabric squares, pin a neutral square to a print/solid fabric square with right sides facing. Using a fabric marker pen and a ruler, mark a line of dots along the diagonal on the back of one of the squares. Using the dotted line as a guide, machine stitch a line ¼" (6 mm) away from it, first to one side, then the other. Cut the squares in half along the dotted line. Open each piece out to give you two triangle squares. Make each triangle square so that the patterned scraps you have selected orientate in the same way within the finished block.

(Image labels:) 9 x 9" (23.8 x 23.8 cm); 4¾ x 4¾" (12.4 x 12.4 cm); Unit A; Unit B; Unit C; Unit D

{03} Piece unit A (make 4)

Pin one 2⅝" (6.7 cm) neutral square to one triangle square. Stitch and press the seam. Pin two triangle squares together, stitch and press the seam. Pin paired units together. Stitch and press the seam to complete unit A.

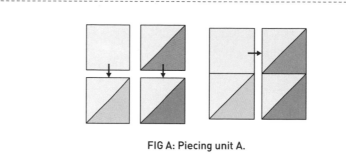

FIG A: Piecing unit A.

{04} Piece unit B (make 6)

Pin two triangle squares together, stitch and press the seam. Repeat to join two more triangle squares. Pin paired units together. Stitch and press the seam to complete unit B.

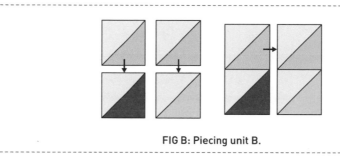

FIG B: Piecing unit B.

{05} Piece unit C (make 2)

Pin one 4¾" (12.4 cm) neutral square to a unit A, stitch together and press the seam. Take another unit A and pin to a unit B, stitch and press the seam. Pin paired units together. Stitch and press the seam to complete unit C.

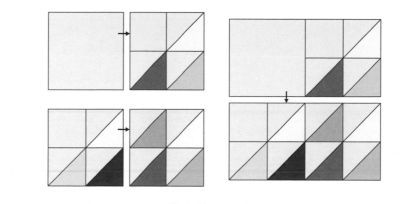

FIG C: Piecing unit C.

{06} Piece unit D (make 1)

Pin a unit B to a unit B, stitch together and press the seam. Join another two B units, then pin the paired units together. Stitch and press the seam to complete unit D.

{07} Complete piecing of block E

Pin one 9 x 9" (23.8 x 23.8 cm) neutral square to a unit C, stitch together and press the seam. Pin a unit D to a unit C, stitch together and press the seam. Pin the paired units together, stitch and press the seam to complete one block.

{08} Piece the broken dishes block

Repeat steps 2 to 7 to make the remaining three blocks required to piece the broken dishes block. Once all four blocks are complete, and noting the orientation of the blocks on the photo opposite, pin two of the finished blocks together. Stitch and press the seam. Join the remaining two blocks, then pin the paired blocks together. Stitch and press seam to complete the broken dishes patchwork top.

{09} Make quilt sandwich and quilt patchwork top

Working on a flat surface, layer up your quilt sandwich with the cotton calico wrong side facing up, batting in the middle, and patchwork on top, right side facing up. Using your preferred method, baste layers together (see page 147). Machine quilt, removing basting as you work. Our cushion was quilted in concentric diamonds working out from the center. Trim layers flush.

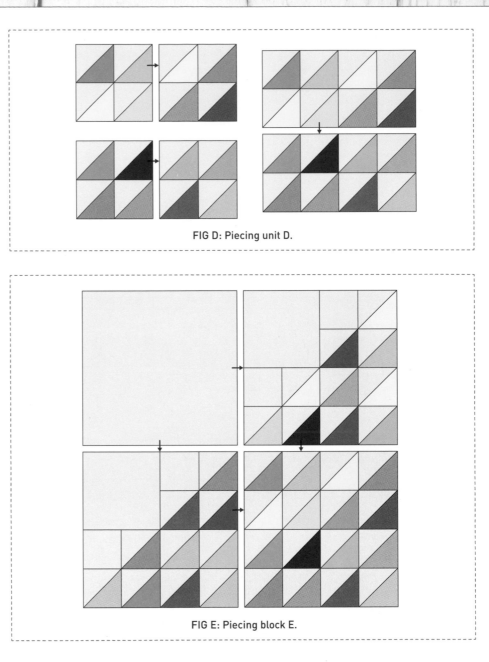

FIG D: Piecing unit D.

FIG E: Piecing block E.

{10} Make the cushion backing

From your backing fabric, cut two rectangles measuring 17½ x 31½" (44.5 x 80 cm). Take one piece and press under a ¼" (6 mm) seam allowance along the long edge. Press an additional 1" (2.5 cm) seam allowance along the same edge. Pin the zipper, wrong side facing up, to the pressed edge, and stitch in place.

Take the second backing fabric piece and press under a ¼" (6 mm) seam allowance along the long edge. Pin hemmed edge to right side of zipper, and stitch in place.

{11} Assemble, bind and finish the cushion

Pin the backing to the quilted patchwork top with wrong sides facing, and trim edges if necessary so they are even.

Cut your binding fabric into 1½" (4 cm) strips and join to make one long strip. Use the joined strip to bind the cushion using the continuous binding technique (see page 152). Insert cushion pad, close the zipper, and prepare to lounge.

Patchwork Story

I do love floor cushions even though nowadays I rarely lay on the floor to watch TV or read! They remind me of my childhood—we didn't have a lot of money, so, with a living room in desperate need of chairs, my crafty mother solved the problem by making an assortment of floor cushions from a variety of fabrics. I remember in particular one made out of faux fur and another sewn from denim with its colorful appliqué patches— the hours my brothers and I spent sprawled on them, watching TV, playing board games and just generally enjoying being kids.

Pinwheels tote bag

{ *The front of this roomy tote bag combines geometric bands of Seminole diamond patchwork, top and bottom, with a center band of spinning pinwheel blocks, cleverly made using flying geese units. Precision patchwork has never looked so pretty.*

MATERIALS

Note: All fabrics are 44–45" (112 cm) wide

1 yard (1 meter) cotton fabric in teal print

¼ yard (0.25 meters) cotton fabric in gold print

½ yard (0.5 meters) cotton fabric in pink floral print

½ yard (0.5 meters) cotton fabric in white

⅛ yard (0.125 meters) cotton fabric in pink square print

1 yard (1 meter) cotton fabric in white floral print for lining

2½ yards (2.5 meters) of 20" (50 cm) wide medium-weight fusible interfacing

Sewing threads to coordinate

One piece of template plastic 18 x 5" (46 x 12.8 cm) for the bag base

SIZE

18 x 15 x 5½" (46 x 38 x 14 cm)

FEATURED TECHNIQUES

- Rotary cutting (page 92)
- Machine piecing (page 98)
- For more on Seminole piecing and variations, see page 110
- For more on flying geese piecing, see page 123

BEFORE YOU BEGIN

Cut all patchwork strips using a rotary cutter, quilter's rule and cutting mat.

When piecing the patchwork, pin and stitch together with right sides facing.

All patchwork piecing seams are a scant ¼" (6 mm). All bag assembly seams are ⅜" (1 cm) seam unless otherwise stated. When pressing patchwork seams, always press to one side. Bag assembly seams should be pressed open.

METHOD

{01} Cut and piece the Seminole diamond bands

These form the top and bottom bands of the front patchwork panel.

First, cut and assemble the panel that will create the larger diamond: cut two strips of white fabric measuring 3 x 25" (7.5 x 63.5 cm) and one strip of pink floral fabric measuring 2 x 25" (5 x 63.5 cm). Stitch the strips together and press the seams toward the white fabric strips. Using a quilter's rule and rotary cutter, trim the right-hand edge of the strip to even out the edges, then cut the rest of the length into 2" (5 cm) strips. Stack the strips and set aside.

Now cut and assemble the panel that will create the smaller diamond: cut two strips of white fabric measuring 3 x 6" (7.5 x 15.5 cm) and one strip of pink square print fabric measuring 1 x 6" (2.5 x 15.5 cm). Stitch the strips together and press the seams toward the white fabric strips. Trim the right-hand edge of the strip to even out the edges, then cut the rest of the length into 1" (2.5 cm) strips, and stack.

Working from your stacks of fabric strips and starting with one wide strip and one narrow strip, line the strips up so that the bottom edge of the small diamond meets the top edge of the large diamond. Stitch together and open out. Take another wide strip and attach it to the narrow strip, lining up the bottom of the large diamond with the top of the small diamond. Continue until all the strips are joined together.

Cut two strips of white fabric measuring 2 x 7¾" (5 x 19.5 cm) and add to each end of the pieced panel, open out and press. Trim the pieced panel into a rectangle. Lay it on the cutting mat with the diamonds aligning with one grid line. Measuring from the center of the diamonds with a quilter's rule, trim the panel width 2" (5 cm) from the center of the diamonds. Turn the panel and repeat. Now trim the panel length to 18½" (47 cm), which should be exactly ¼" (6 mm) from the edge of the last diamond on each side.

Make a second diamond panel in exactly the same way.

{02} Cut and piece the flying geese pinwheel blocks

These form the middle band of the front patchwork panel. Cut the following pieces from your fabrics:

From gold print fabric:
Four squares measuring 2½ x 2½" (6.25 x 6.25 cm)

From pink floral print fabric:
Two squares measuring 2½ x 2½" (6.25 x 6.25 cm)

From white fabric:
12 squares measuring 2 x 2" (5 x 5 cm)
12 rectangles measuring 3 x 1¾" (7.5 x 4.5 cm)

From teal print fabric:
Four strips measuring 1 x 6" (2.5 x 15.5 cm)

Cut each of the gold print, pink floral and white squares in half on the diagonal (fig A).

Make the flying geese units using scant ¼" (6 mm) seams. Match the long edge of a white triangle to the short edge of a colored triangle, keeping the bottom edges flush. Stitch, open out, and press seam toward the white fabric (fig B). Join a white triangle to the other short edge of the colored triangle in the same way to complete the flying geese unit (fig C). Make eight gold flying geese units and four pink.

Stitch a white rectangle to the top of each flying geese unit to create a square (fig D). Lay out the squares in a pinwheel pattern, making two gold flying geese pinwheel blocks and one pink (see note on page 44). For each block, stitch the two bottom squares together, then stitch the two top squares together and press seams (fig E); join the rectangles together to create the pinwheel block, trimming any seams that overlap the edges (fig F).

Lay the three finished pinwheel blocks out in order, with the pink block in the middle. Working from left to right, stitch one teal print strip to the left-hand side of the first gold pinwheel, then stitch one strip to the right-hand side. Join the left-hand edge of the pink pinwheel, then stitch another teal print strip to the right-hand side of the pink pinwheel.

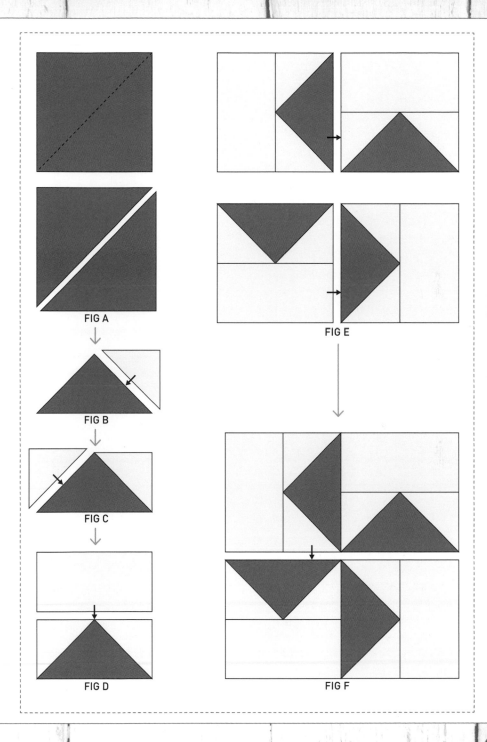

FIG A

FIG B

FIG C

FIG D

FIG E

FIG F

Sew on the second gold pinwheel and stitch the final teal strip to the right-hand side. Press seams.

{03} Assemble the front panel of the bag

Check all three bands are the same length, trimming if not. Cut four strips of teal print fabric each measuring 18½ x 1" (47 x 2.5 cm). Referring to the photo below, stitch a teal strip to the top and bottom of the pinwheel band. Stitch a Seminole diamond band to the top and bottom of these teal strips. Add the last two teal strips to the top and bottom of the panel. Set aside.

Note

You can make all three pinwheel blocks to face the same way working from the diagrams on page 43, which show the piecing of the middle pinwheel square using the pink triangles. If, however, you prefer the gold pinwheels to face the opposite direction as on the finished panel, refer to the photo above to flip the final assembly of the squares in figs E and F.

{04} Cut and prepare remaining pieces required for bag assembly

Cut the following pieces.
From the teal print fabric:
Two pieces measuring 15½ x 6" (39.5 x 15.5 cm) for the side panels
Two pieces measuring 8 x 6" (20.3 x 15.5 cm) for the side pockets
One piece measuring 18½ x 15½" (47 x 39.5 cm) for the back panel
One piece measuring 18½ x 6" (47 x 15.5 cm) for the bottom panel

From the white floral print lining fabric:
Two pieces measuring 15½ x 6" (39.5 x 15.5 cm) for lining side panels
Two pieces measuring 18½ x 15½" (47 x 39.5 cm) for lining front and back panels
One piece measuring 18½ x 6" (47 x 15.5 cm) for lining base panel
Two pieces measuring 3 x 30" (7.5 x 76 cm) for the shoulder straps outer side

From the pink floral print fabric:
One piece measuring 8 x 18½" (20.3 x 47 cm) for the inner pocket
Two pieces measuring 3 x 30" (7.5 x 76 cm) for the shoulder strap underside

From the gold print fabric:
One piece measuring 8½ x 18½" (21.6 x 47 cm) for inner pocket lining
Two pieces measuring 8½ x 6" (21.6 x 15.5 cm) for the outer pocket linings

From the medium-weight fusible interfacing:
Two pieces measuring 15½ x 6" (39.5 x 15.5 cm) for the side panels
Two pieces measuring 18½ x 15½" (47 x 39 cm) piece for the front and back panels
One piece measuring 18½ x 6" (47 x 15.5 cm) for the base panel
Two pieces measuring 8 x 6" (20.3 x 15.5 cm) for the side pockets
Two pieces measuring 3 x 30" (7.5 x 76 cm) for the shoulder straps

Following the manufacturer's instructions, press fusible interfacing to the front and back panels, side panels, base panels, side pockets, and the pink floral shoulder straps.

Patchwork Story

Seminole patchwork is a technique that is relatively new to me, but the way the geometric patterns emerge as the fabric strips are sewn together makes my heart sing at the sewing machine. I hope you'll feel the same excitement as you watch the patterns unfold when you create this lovely roomy tote bag. Creating a patchwork piece is always a labor of love—the time spent choosing, cutting and piecing always carries a little bit of the maker with it wherever it goes.

{05} Assemble back of bag, pockets and inner lining

Matching the top edges and with right sides facing, stitch the gold outer pocket linings to the teal side pockets using a ¼" (6 mm) seam allowance. Fold the lining to the inside and press, matching the bottom edges together, which should leave a small strip of gold fabric showing on the outside of the pocket. Topstitch to finish (see note on page 46).

Baste the lined pockets to the teal side panels, matching edges at sides and base. Stitch the side panels to each side of the front patchwork panel, leaving ⅜" (1 cm) open at the bottom edge. Stitch the back panel to the side panels, again leaving ⅜" (1 cm) open on the bottom edge. Pin the teal base panel to the bottom edge of the assembled bag, matching the side seams to the corners of the base panel (see photo below)—the openings will allow the sides to fit around the corners of the bottom panel. Stitch in place.

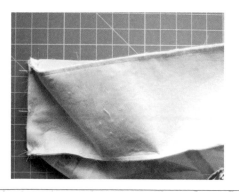

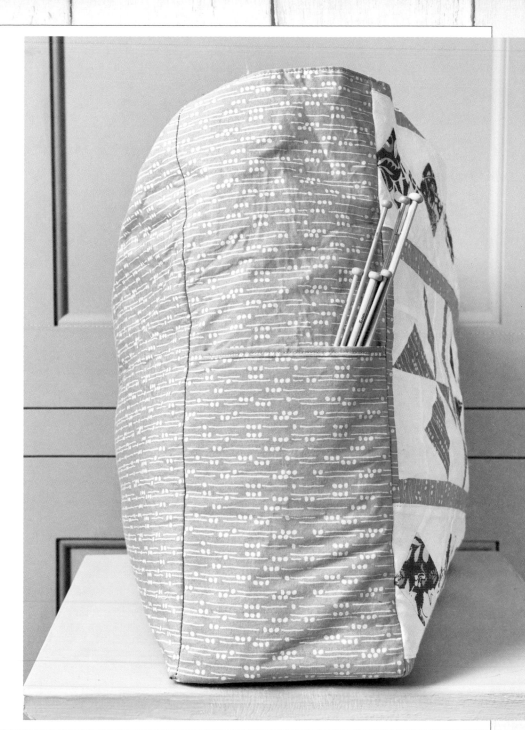

{06} Make the bag straps

Pair up the interfaced shoulder straps with the white floral print shoulder straps with right sides facing, and stitch together along long edges. Turn right side out and press. Topstitch along the stitched edges.

Pin and baste the straps to the top edge of the front and back panels, 3" (7.5 cm) from each side, matching the raw edges, so that the white floral side faces the right side of the front and back panels.

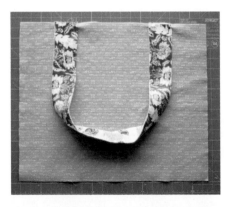

{07} Assemble the bag lining and finish

Matching the top edges and with right sides facing, stitch the inner pocket (pink) to the inner pocket lining (gold) using a ¼" (6 mm) seam allowance. Fold the lining to the inside. Press, matching the bottom edges together, which should leave a small strip of gold fabric showing on the outside of the pocket. Topstitch to finish. Baste the pocket to the inner back panel. Add a vertical line of stitching about 5" (13 cm) from each outer edge to create smaller pockets.

Stitch the lining side panels to the lining front and back panels, then attach to the lining base, referring to step 5 for details.

Keeping the lining with right sides facing inward, slip the outer bag inside the lining, matching at all corners. Stitch along the top edge of the bag, starting at the back shoulder strap and leaving the space between the straps open. Turn the bag right side out through the opening. Press, taking care to turn the raw edges under at the opening.

Slip the template plastic into the bag base and topstitch around the top edge of the bag to close the opening and finish. Go shopping!

LEAH FARQUHARSON

Leah Farquharson is a wife, mother and business owner of lovely handmade things, living in Miami, Florida. She is passionate about the power of handmade and its ability to change our modern world. Her designs are typically influenced by traditional American crafting or fashion, with a modern vintage feel. You can see more of her thoughts, recipes and handmade goods at bluebirdchic.com.

Note

Topstitching is an extra row of stitching on the outside of the project along or near the finished edge. On the tote bag, it is used to keep the lining edging of the pocket in place and to neaten the bag straps. It is important to make sure that your stitching line is nice and even.

Log cabin cushion

This sweet log cabin cushion cover is a great way to use up small fabric scraps or material off-cuts. Made from vintage bed linens, its gelato color palette makes any space prettier, and it is trimmed with pom-pom braid for extra whimsy. Quilted as you go and with an envelope back closure, it's so easy to make too.

DESIGNED BY CINTIA GONZALEZ

MATERIALS

Assorted pastel-colored fabrics with a minimum width of 2⅜–2¾" (6–7 cm), ranging from 2¾–15¾" (7–40 cm) in length for the patchwork (see step 1 for exact measurements)

One piece of cotton calico 15¾in x 15¾" (40 x 40 cm) for the lining

Two pieces of cotton 12 x 15¾" (30 x 40 cm) for the backing

One piece of cotton quilt batting 15¾in x 15¾" (40 x 40 cm)

Pom-pom trim 48" (120 cm)

Cushion insert 16" (40.5 cm)

White sewing thread

Disappearing marker pen

SIZE

14½ x 14½" (37 x 37 cm)

FEATURED TECHNIQUES

- Machine quilting: straight lines (page 149)
- For more on log cabin piecing and variations, see page 107

BEFORE YOU BEGIN

Prewash and press fabrics before use as necessary: this is particularly important if you are using vintage fabrics as these may have dyes that run when washed.

For clean accurate cutting measurements, use a rotary cutter, quilter's rule and cutting mat to cut your strips.

All seam allowances are ⅜" (1 cm) unless otherwise stated. Use of a walking foot (page 88) is recommended.

By choosing an insert larger than your finished cover size, your cushion will look nicely plump—when used, the insert fillings do tend to flatten out.

Patchwork Story

Quilt-as-you-go patchwork piecing takes the scary part out of quilting for me, especially for big projects. As the block grows the finished look appears magically before your eyes and allows you to create a heavily quilted effect without the dread of all that finishing work at the end. Don't stop at a cushion—why not join several of these pre-quilted blocks and turn them into a quilt?

METHOD

{01} Cut your patchwork fabrics

Cut your patchwork pieces from your chosen fabrics. The center of the log cabin patchwork is a 2¾" (7 cm) square and the strips that radiate out from the center square in a clockwise direction are all 2⅜" (6 cm) wide. You can cut them to length as you go or precut them using the following measurements as your guide.

Center	2¾" (7 cm) square
Strip 1	2¾" (7 cm)
Strips 2 and 3	4¼" (11 cm)
Strips 4 and 5	5¾" (15 cm)
Strips 6 and 7	7½" (19 cm)
Strips 8 and 9	9" (23 cm)
Strips 10 and 11	10½" (27 cm)
Strips 12 and 13	12¼" (31 cm)
Strips 14 and 15	13¾" (35 cm)
Strip 16	15¼" (39 cm)

{02} Piece and quilt the log cabin patchwork

Note: Work from the patchwork piecing diagram for order of piecing, and use a walking foot on your sewing machine. Trim threads after each piecing step.

Take your batting square and find the center by lightly ruling two lines from opposite corners with your disappearing marker pen that intersect in the center to mark an X.

Lay the batting over the calico lining fabric so that edges align. Place the center patchwork fabric square in the center of the batting so that the corners touch the ruled guidelines.

Machine quilt straight parallel lines ⅜" (1 cm) apart over the center square.

Position the central square and begin to quilt-as-you-go.

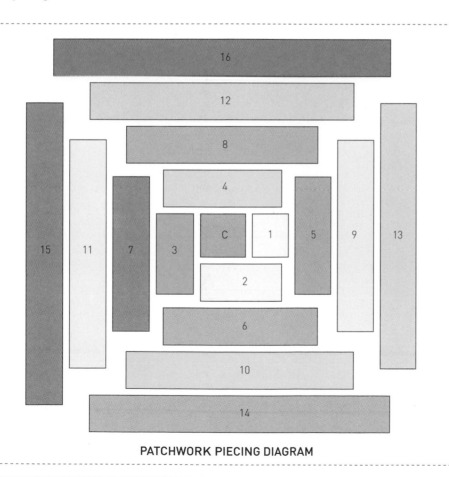

PATCHWORK PIECING DIAGRAM

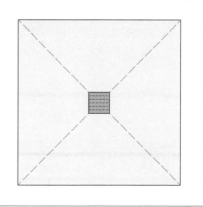

Lay strip 1 (right side facing down) over the center square and sew a ⅜" (1 cm) seam on the right-hand edge. Flip over, press and quilt with straight parallel lines that run perpendicular to center square (see photos below).

Lay strip 2 over the center square and strip 1, sew seam, flip and quilt. Continue with all strips, working in a clockwise direction until you reach the edge of the batting. Trim the patchwork panel to neaten and to make it as close to 15¾" (40 cm) square as possible.

The finished log cabin block, trimmed up and ready for cushion assembly.

Following the patchwork piecing diagram on page 49, lay each fabric piece in turn, right sides together. Sew seam, flip over, and quilt, alternating between horizontal and vertical lines of parellel stitching.

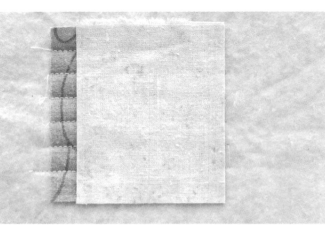

{03} Assemble the cushion

Change back to the standard foot on your sewing machine and sew a double-fold hem along one long side of both of the backing pieces: fold under ⅜" (1 cm), press with wrong sides facing, then fold over ⅜" (1 cm) again to enclose the raw edge; pin and sew about ⅛" (3 mm) from the edge of the fold.

Pin the pom-pom trim to the patchwork panel, lining up the edge of the trim to the edge of the panel with pom-poms facing in. Starting and finishing on a corner, stitch in place sewing as close to the edge of the trim as possible.

Lay your top patchwork panel right side facing up. Lay the back panels on top with right sides facing down, so that the raw edges line up with the sides of the top panel and the hemmed edges overlap by about 5½" (14 cm) to create an envelope opening. Pin around the edges (note: the pom-poms should be sandwiched in between the layers and may be a little lumpy).

Machine stitch around the outer edge allowing for a ⅜" (1 cm) seam allowance (or as close as you can get to the pom-poms). Sew one side at a time and readjust pins and pom-poms if required. Clip the corners and zigzag raw edges of seams to prevent fraying. Turn out and carefully stuff cushion through envelope backing. Take a seat!

Clamshell iPad sleeve

{ A simple repeated design in eye-catching fabrics is the perfect way to dress up your tablet device. Using an easy needle-turn appliqué technique to stitch the gentle curves of the clamshell piecing, you can make a delightful and useful cover for your iPad. Make one for you and one for a friend, or create smaller sleeves for your sun glasses or mobile phone.

MATERIALS

49 scraps of 100% quilting-weight cotton fabric each at least 3 x 3" (7.5 x 7.5 cm) for the clamshell patchwork

One piece of cotton calico 9 x 11¼" (22.8 x 28.5 cm) for foundation

One piece of polka dot cotton fabric 9 x 11¼" (22.8 x 28.5 cm) for backing

Two pieces of solid cotton fabric 9 x 11¼" (22.8 x 28.5 cm) for the lining

Two pieces of low-loft cotton batting 9 x 11¼" (22.8 x 28.5 cm)

Milliner's needle and sewing thread

Cotton perlé embroidery floss size 8

Small length of elastic cording or ribbon

One button

Disappearing marker, temporary basting spray (optional) and fabric glue stick

SIZE

8½ x 10" (21.5 x 25.5 cm)

FEATURED TECHNIQUES

- Making templates (page 90)
- Turned-edge hand appliqué (page 137)
- Basic hand stitches (page 95)
- For more on clamshell piecing and variations, see page 130

BEFORE YOU BEGIN

Prewash and press fabrics before use as necessary: this is particularly important if you are using vintage fabrics as these may have dyes that run when washed.

Make a template for the clamshell (page 154) from template plastic. (The template does not include a seam allowance.)

All seams are ¼" (6 mm) unless otherwise stated.

Patchwork Story

My patchwork story began more than 25 years ago when, as a stay-at-home mother with young children looking for a creative outlet, I picked up a quilting pattern. I am self-taught and through years of practice, success and failure, my quilting style has taken shape. I love traditional blocks and combine them with modern fabrics and big stitch quilting to update the classics with a touch of whimsy. For the iPad sleeve I chose fun, bright fabrics with cute kitschy designs, polka dots and gingham.

METHOD

{01} Mark the grid onto the foundation calico

Using a pencil and ruler, mark the calico up with an even grid, four squares across and five rows down, where each square in the grid measures 2¼ x 2¼" (5.7 x 5.7 cm). As well as providing a guide for the placing of the clamshells, the calico grid will also provide a foundation for the appliqué.

{02} Cut clamshell fabric pieces

Use the clamshell template to mark out 49 clamshells from scrap fabrics. Using a disappearing marker pen or tailor's chalk, trace around the shape onto the right side of fabric squares and cut out allowing for a ¼" (6 mm) seam allowance around the curved part of the shape. **Do not** leave a seam allowance on the tip of the clamshell, but cut this part of the shape directly on the drawn line (see photo below left).

{03} Appliqué the first row of clamshell patchwork

Take your first clamshell piece and use the fabric glue stick to dab a little glue on the wrong side. Beginning at the top left-hand side of the calico grid, place the clamshell in the first square so that the sides of the curved drawn line meet the edge of the calico and the grid line. Using a milliner's needle, sewing thread and whipstitch, appliqué the top curve of the clamshell to the calico foundation by hand. **Do not** appliqué the scooped out (concave) sections on either side of the clamshell tip, but use the side of your needle to turn under the seam allowance at the marked curve as you work your way around the top of the shape. Repeat to stitch a clamshell in each square of row 1 (see photo below).

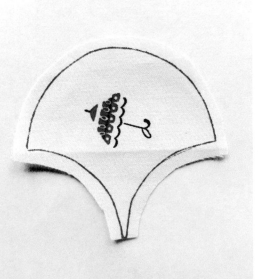

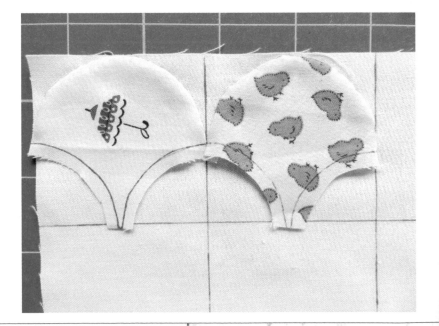

{04} Appliqué remaining rows of clamshell patchwork

The clamshells are staggered in row 2. Cut one clamshell shape in half lengthwise and glue in place at the beginning of row 2—see photos below (the grid lines will bisect the next full clamshell shape and row 2 will end with a half clamshell shape).

Continue working rows of staggered clamshells until you reach the end of the calico grid, remembering only to stitch down the top curved part of the shapes. *Note: On the final row, the bottom tips of the clamshells will hang over the edge of the foundation piece.*

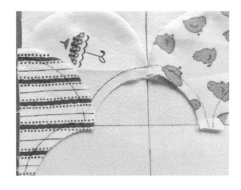

{05} Trim patchwork panel and outline stitch

Turn the patchwork over to the wrong side and trim the bottom row so that it is even with the calico foundation. Turn back to the right side and trim ¾" (2 cm) from the top row—see photo above. Use a coordinating color of cotton perlé embroidery floss and an embroidery needle to outline the clamshell curves with running stitch.

{06} Assemble the iPad sleeve

Cut one piece of backing fabric, two pieces of lining fabric and two pieces of batting the same size as the patchwork front, trimming as necessary. Secure a piece of batting to the wrong side of both the patchwork front and the backing fabric, working basting stitches close to the edges (alternatively, use temporary basting spray).

Fold a piece of ribbon or elastic cording in half, and place centrally along the top edge of the backing fabric (right side facing), so that the loop is facing down into the center of the fabric (do make sure that the loop is large enough to accommodate your button). Baste in place.

Place a lining piece together with the patchwork front with right sides facing and stitch together along the top short edge. Repeat to attach the remaining lining piece to the backing fabric. Fold open the joined fabric pieces and lay the backing fabric/lining on top of the patchwork front/lining with right sides facing. Pin in place matching the seams on both sides where the lining and sleeve meet, allowing for a 3" (7.5 cm) opening on the bottom (short) edge of the lining. Begin stitching at one side of the opening and sew all the way around to the other side of the opening, reverse stitching at the beginning and end and taking care to pull the pins out as you stitch.

Turn the sleeve right side out through the opening. Stitch the opening in the lining closed and push the lining into the sleeve to create a pocket. Press well. Topstitch around the sleeve opening with a coordinating thread, and stitch your button to the center front of the sleeve to finish.

Mini hexies apron

{ Become a domestic goddess with this oh-so-pretty natural linen apron trimmed with a panel of miniature English paper-pieced hexagons. If you have an overflowing box of fabric off-cuts, this technique is a lovely way to use up small scraps of all your favorites. You can make the patchwork band on this apron in any colors you like—just let your remnants guide you.

MATERIALS

One piece of linen fabric 23½ x 17⅝" (60 x 45 cm) for the apron front

1 yard (1 meter) of 44–45" (112 cm) wide printed fabric for the apron lining, waistband, and ties

Scraps of patterned fabric for the patchwork panel

25½" (65 cm) length of lace

Sewing thread to match linen fabric

Embroidery thread

Temporary basting spray

SIZE

About 21¼ x 18" (54 x 46 cm) (excluding waistband ties)

FEATURED TECHNIQUES

- Making templates (page 90)
- English paper piecing (page 94)
- Basic hand stitches (page 95)
- Hand quilting (page 148)

BEFORE YOU BEGIN

Prewash and press fabrics before use as necessary: this is important if you are using vintage fabrics as these may have dyes that run when washed.

Referring to the hexagon template provided (see page 156), note that the inner line is for cutting the paper templates that remain inside the fabric pieces until they are all stitched together, and the outer line is for cutting the fabric scraps so includes seam allowances. Use the template to make a plastic window template for cutting perfectly proportioned paper and fabric hexagons time and time again (see page 94).

Once you have cut the pieces for the apron lining, waistband, and ties from your 1 yard (1 meter) of patterned fabric, use leftovers to cut a few of the hexies to give your apron a coordinated look.

All seams are ¼" (6 mm) unless otherwise stated.

METHOD

{01} Cut your fabrics

Cut the following pieces:

From your patterned fabric:

One rectangle measuring 23½ x 20" (60 x 50 cm) for the apron lining

One rectangle measuring 20 x 5¾" (50 x 15 cm) for the waistband

Two strips measuring 39¼ x 5¾" (100 x 15 cm) for the ties

From your fabric scraps:

37 hexagons using the larger (outer) hexagon template

{02} Piece and position the mini hexies panel

Use the smaller (inner) hexagon template to cut 37 hexagons from paper, one for each fabric hexagon. Following the instructions on page 94, center a paper hexagon on the wrong side of each fabric hexagon, fold over the seam allowance and stitch in place. Hand stitch the prepared hexagons together to make a panel two hexagons deep.

Gently press the completed hexie panel on the reverse, then carefully remove the paper templates from the fabric hexagons using a pin (photo 1). Apply temporary basting spray to the back of the hexie panel and position it 2" (5 cm) from the bottom edge of the linen rectangle. Pin well, then whipstitch in place by hand (photo 2).

To highlight the hexie panel, hand quilt a simple running stitch border a little way away from the edge, top and bottom, using an embroidery floss in the color of your choosing (photo 3).

{03} Attach lining to the apron front

Place the decorated apron front and the lining fabric right sides together, lining them up along the bottom edge Pin and machine stitch, then press the seam open. Working on the front of the joined fabric panel, pin and stitch the lace along the join. Using a water-erasable pen, draw a line on the linen fabric ³⁄₈" (1 cm) above the lace, then hand

PHOTO 1

PHOTO 2

PHOTO 3

PHOTO 4

quilt a line of running stitches along it. Once the running stitch is complete, spray with water to make the pen line disappear.

Fold the joined fabric panel with right sides together, this time lining up the top edges but making sure that the patterned lining fabric shows equally all the way along the bottom edge of the front. Smooth the fabric out carefully and trim the side edges to neaten (this will remove the extra half hexagon from the bottom row of the hexie panel). Pin and machine stitch along each side edge. Turn right sides out and press, lining up the edges neatly. Topstitch along the sides, stopping just before the hexie panel—photo 4 (do not topstitch beneath the panel).

{04} Create the pleats

Working on the front of the apron at the top right-hand edge and following photo 5 sequence below, use pins to mark 5¾" (15 cm) and 7½" (19 cm) from the edge. Fold the fabric so that the pins meet to make an outward facing pleat. Pin, then stitch the pleat in place. Repeat to make a mirror-image pleat on the top left-hand side. Press the pleats. Trim, pin, then stitch along the top of the apron close to the edge, to keep the apron front and lining nicely together.

PHOTO 5

{05} Make the waistband and ties

Machine stitch the short edges of the waistband to the short edges of the ties to make one long strip with the waistband section in the center. Press seams open.

Lay the lined apron onto the joined waistband/ties strip so that the apron front is lying on the right side of the waistband/ties strip, lining up the top edges. Machine stitch together using a ½" (1.3 cm) seam allowance.

Working on the front side of the apron, fold the waistband/ties strip right sides together matching the long edges. Pin and stitch, leaving the center waistband area open (see photo below). Turn the ties right side out and press neatly.

Fold and press the unsewn center of the waistband under on the back of the apron so that it covers the stitched line (see photo right). Place a few pins to hold it in position. Turn the apron over to pin the waistband well from the front, then machine stitch close to the edge. Put your pretty new apron on, tie a bow and get baking!

Patchwork Story

I have such fond memories as a little girl, of stitching fabric hexagons with my mum. Diving into her fabric scraps was like heaven to me, better even than a trip to the sweet shop! Bitten by the bug, I have adored patchwork ever since. These days, there is nothing I love more than getting comfy on the sofa in the evening, a little pile of ready-cut hexies by my side, needle and thread in hand, a good film on the TV, and maybe a little tipple of something nice.

JOOLES
OF SEW SWEET VIOLET

Jooles, a lover of sewing, craftiness and eating cake, lives in West Sussex, U.K. with Mr Sweet and their two gorgeous grown-up children. A homebody at heart, she loves nothing more than a whole day spent in her sewing room stitching away in her own sweet time. For her blog see sewsweetviolet.blogspot.com or discover more of her work at sewsweetviolet.etsy.com or www.notonthehighstreet.com/sewsweetviolet.

Snail's trail quilt

The snail's trail block is great for beginners, and although it may look as if it has very complex curves, it is made up of squares and triangles so it is quite simple to piece. By carefully selecting the fabrics you use, you can really emphasize the spiraling effect created when the blocks are joined together. This traditional pattern is sure to feel at home in even the most modern setting.

DESIGNED BY MALKA DUBRAWSKY

MATERIALS

Note: All fabrics are 44–45" (112 cm) wide

2 yards (2 meters) white or cream cotton fabric

2 yards (2 meters) printed cotton fabric in mixed patterns

4 yards (3.75 meters) wide coordinated cotton fabric for backing

⅓ yard (0.3 meter) of coordinated cotton fabric for binding

Cotton batting measuring at least 70 x 70" (178 x 178 cm)

Sewing thread in coordinating colors

SIZE

65 x 65" (165 x 165 cm)

FEATURED TECHNIQUES

- Machine piecing (page 98)
- Four-patch (page 114)
- Joining blocks without sashing (page 142)
- Making a quilt sandwich (page 146)
- Machine quilting (page 149)
- Continuous binding (page 152)
- For more on snail's trail piecing and variations, see page 120

BEFORE YOU BEGIN

Prewash and press fabrics before use as necessary: this is particularly important if you are using vintage fabrics as these may have dyes that run when washed.

For accurate cutting of the patchwork pieces, use of a rotary cutter, quilter's rule and cutting mat is recommended.

When piecing, pin and stitch together with right sides facing. **All seams are ¼" (6 mm) unless otherwise stated.** Unless otherwise directed, press all seams to one side, alternating sides where seams intersect.

METHOD

{01} Cut your patchwork fabrics

Cut the following pieces:

From white or cream cotton fabric:
32 squares 3½ x 3½" (8.9 x 8.9 cm)
16 squares 5 x 5" (12.7 x 12.7 cm)
16 squares 6¾ x 6¾" (17 x 17 cm)
16 squares 8⅞ x 8⅞" (22.6 x 22.6 cm)

From your printed cotton fabric in mixed patterns:
32 squares 3½ x 3½" (8.9 x 8.9 cm)
16 squares 5 x 5" (12.7 x 12.7 cm)
16 squares 6¾ x 6¾" (17 x 17 cm)
16 squares 8⅞ x 8⅞" (22.6 x 22.6 cm)

Use a quilter's rule to cut all but the 3½" (8.9 cm) squares into triangles.

{02} Make the snail's trail block (make 16)

Using the remaining 3½ x 3½" (8.9 x 8.9 cm) squares, make a four-patch unit—see fig A and page 114.

Pin white/cream 5" (12.7 cm) triangles to opposite edges of the center square, sew and press the seams (fig B). Join same-size print triangles in the same way (fig C).

Referring to the snail's trail block photo on page 64 for placing of the white/cream and print triangles,

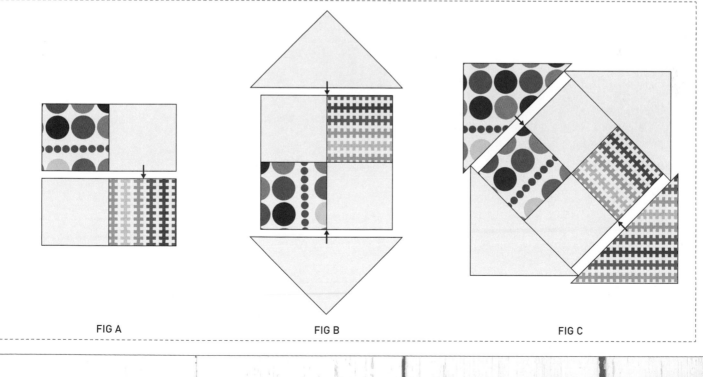

FIG A   FIG B   FIG C

continue to add first the 6¾" (17 cm) triangles, then the 8⅞" (22.6 cm) triangles in the same way.

{03} Lay out and sew the blocks together into rows
Check all of your blocks are the same size. Working on a clean floor and using the quilt layout diagram opposite as a guide, lay out the finished blocks in four rows of four. When you are happy with the layout, join the blocks together. Starting with row 1, take the first two blocks, pin and sew together and press seam. Repeat to join the second pair of blocks. Pin the sewn pairs together, sew and press seam.

Repeat to join the blocks in the remaining three rows.

{04} Sew the rows together
Pin rows 1 and 2 together, sew and press seam. Continue in the same way to add one row at a time— row 3 to row 2, then row 4 to row 3.

{05} Make quilt sandwich and quilt patchwork top
From your backing fabric, cut two pieces measuring 72" (183 cm)

The finished snail's trail block. When the completed blocks are laid out into their setting pattern, the spiraling effect is even more obvious (see quilt layout diagram opposite).

by the full width of the fabric. Pin together along one long edge with right sides facing. Sew, then press the seam open.

Working on a clean, flat surface, layer up your quilt sandwich as follows: backing fabric wrong side facing up, batting in the middle, and quilt top right side facing up. Using your preferred method (see page 146), baste layers together. Machine or hand quilt, removing basting as you work. For the quilt shown, a fairly free spiral pattern was quilted across the quilt with quilting lines spaced about ¼" (6 mm) apart. Once the quilting is complete, trim layers flush.

{06} Assemble, bind and finish

Cut your binding fabric into 1½" (4 cm) strips and join to make one long strip (see page 151). Use the strip to bind the quilt using the continuous binding technique (see page 152) for single binding, turning the binding to the back to finish by hand, maintaining a ¼" (5 mm) seam allowance.

QUILT LAYOUT DIAGRAM

Starting at the point where four blocks join to create the secondary diamond pattern, fairly free lines of machine quilting spiral out to echo the spiraling arms of the snail's trail design.

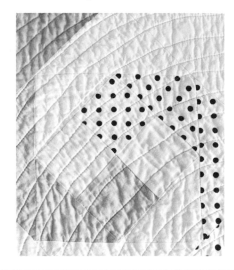

Seminole diamond camera case

This stylish little bag is a simple way to travel light on a day out. With its generous shoulder strap, you can go hands-free—it is just the right size to carry a camera along with your smart phone. It also has a small inner pocket to keep your debit or credit card safe. Best of all, the fabrics have been waterproofed with iron-on vinyl for all-weather protection.

MATERIALS

Note: All fabrics are 44–45" (112 cm) wide

¼ yard (0.25 meters) cotton fabric in gray print

¼ yard (0.25 meters) cotton fabric in light blue print

¼ yard (0.25 meters) cotton fabric in navy blue print

⅛ yard (0.125 meters) cotton fabric in light orange print

⅛ yard (0.125 meters) cotton fabric in multicolored print

Medium-weight fusible interfacing about 24 x 5" (60 x 13 cm)

One packet of iron-on vinyl (HeatnBond)

Zipper longer than 11½" (29 cm)

Two metal hinge close clasps for strap

Sewing thread

Teflon presser foot attachment for the sewing machine

SIZE

About 6½ x 4" (16 x 9.5 cm)

FEATURED TECHNIQUES

- Machine piecing (page 98)
- For more on Seminole piecing and variations, see page 110

BEFORE YOU BEGIN

Prewash and press fabrics before use as necessary. Cut all strips using a cutting mat, rotary cutter and quilter's rule.

For advice on working with iron-on vinyl see page 69.

All seams are scant ¼" (6 mm) unless otherwise stated. All fabrics are stitched right sides together. All seams are pressed to one side.

Use a Teflon presser foot to stitch all vinyl-backed fabric pieces.

DESIGNED BY
LEAH FARQUHARSON

METHOD

{01} Cut the fabrics for the patchwork

The front of the camera bag is formed from bands of Seminole diamonds. Cut the following strips from your fabrics working across the full fabric width:

One strip of light blue print fabric measuring 1½" (3.8 cm)

One strip of navy blue print fabric measuring 1½" (3.8 cm)

One strip of light orange print fabric measuring 1½" (3.8 cm)

One strip of gray print fabric measuring 1½" (3.8 cm)

One strip of gray print fabric measuring 3" (7.5 cm)

Take each strip and trim into 7" (18 cm) lengths. Set aside the narrow gray lengths for the time being.

{02} Make the Seminole diamond front panel

You will need to piece the fabric lengths together, working along the long edges (7"/18 cm) to make two joined fabric bands from which strips will be cut and rejoined to make the distinctive diamond pattern.

To make the first joined fabric band, join a wide gray fabric strip to a light blue fabric strip, then add a light orange strip, a navy blue strip and finish with a wide gray strip and press. Working on a cutting mat, use a quilter's rule and rotary cutter to trim the right-hand edge of the joined fabric band to even out the

edges, then cut four strips from it measuring 1½" (3.8 cm) wide.

To make the second joined fabric band, join a wide gray fabric strip to a light blue fabric strip, then add a light orange strip, a light blue strip and finish with a wide gray strip. Press and trim as before, then cut just one 1½" (3.8 cm) wide strip from it for the center of the diamond band (you can use the remainder to experiment with other Seminole designs—see page 110).

Referring to photo (a) below, lay out the joined strips to make the patchwork, matching seams neatly and adding the set aside narrow gray strips to the far left- and far right-hand sides. Stitch the strips together and press.

Lining the center of the orange diamond up on the cutting mat grid (b), trim to 6¾ x 4⅛" (17 x 10.5 cm). Set aside the diamond panel.

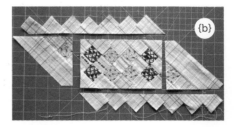

{03} Cut and prepare remaining bag fabrics

Cut the fabric for the remainder of the outer bag as follows:

From the gray print fabric:

Two pieces 1¼ x 2" (3.2 x 5.5 cm) for the side tabs

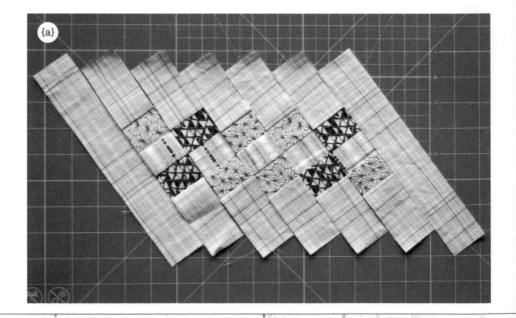

One piece 6¾ x 4⅛" (17 x 10.5 cm) for the back panel
Two pieces 1 x 11½" (2.5 x 29 cm) for the top side panels

From the multicolored fabric:
One piece 2 x 10¼" (5.3 x 26 cm) for the base side panel

From the fusible vinyl:
Two pieces 6¾ x 4⅛" (17 x 10.5 cm) for the back and front (patchwork) panels
Two pieces 1 x 11½" (2.5 x 29 cm) piece for the top side panels
One piece 2 x 10¼" (5.3 x 26 cm) for the base side panel

Following the manufacturer's instructions, add the vinyl to all of the outer pieces, including the set aside patchwork panel.

Now cut the fabric pieces for the bag lining, which are **not** vinyl-backed:
From the light blue fabric:
Two pieces 6¾ x 4⅛" (17 x 10.5 cm) for lining back and front
Two pieces 1 x 11½" (2.5 x 29 cm) for lining top side panels
One piece 2 x 10¼" (5.3 x 26 cm) for lining base side panel

From the navy blue fabric:
One piece 6¾ x 3½" (17 x 9 cm) for the inner pocket

{04} Prepare the side panel
Trim your zipper to the required length by measuring and marking 11½" (29 cm) from the opening end, stitching across the zipper teeth several times to secure, and trimming excess. Sew each top side panel strip in turn to the trimmed zipper, placing the strip with right side facing down on top of the zipper, and fold open.

To make the side tabs that attach the strap, fold each side tab strip in half lengthwise with right sides together and stitch along the long edge. Turn right side out and topstitch along the edge. Fold so that the raw edges meet and stitch

a tab to each end of the zipper. See photo (c) below.

With right sides facing, pin the base side strip to the either end of the top side panel and stitch to form a loop. Turn the fabric loop through to the right side and topstitch to finish.

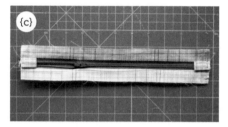
{c}

Working with iron-on vinyl

Iron-on vinyl gives you the opportunity to transform your favorite fabrics into hardwearing and waterproof oilcloth. Leah shares her tips for getting the best results with this innovative product.

"I cut the oilcloth pieces just very slightly smaller than my fabric pieces. The uncovered edges were hidden within the seams once the pieces were sewn, and I found it much easier to fuse them together. It was easy to cut

the roll using my cutting mat, rotary cutter and quilter's rule.

Instead of fusing the product to each of the fabrics used to piece the patchwork, I chose to complete the patchwork first and fuse the oilcloth to the finished panel. Not only did this save me time, it also made the seams waterproof. Don't forget to turn the steam off on your iron before pressing oilcloth– a mistake I often make!"

{05} Assemble the outer bag

Center the zipper on top of the set aside front (patchwork) panel, right sides together, and pin. Clip small slits in the fabric of the side/zipper piece so that it will wrap around the corner of the front panel. Stitch, easing the side piece when going around corners. See photo (d) below.

Open the zipper at least halfway, and pin the side panel to the back panel as before. Stitch, and then clip the corners.

{06} Make the bag lining

First make the inner pocket. Take the piece of navy blue fabric and fold under one long edge by ¼" (6 mm) and press. Fold under by another ¼" (6 mm), press once again and topstitch. Baste the prepared pocket to the lining back, matching the raw edges, and set aside.

Continue to make the lining. Take the light blue lining top side panel strips and prepare by folding a ¼" (6 mm) double hem along one edge (as you did for the inner pocket), topstitching to finish. Referring to the photo, pin the top side panel strips to the lining base side panel, leaving a gap in the middle of each. Stitch to join the lining side panel. See photo (e), top right.

To complete the lining, pin one edge of the side panel to the lining front panel, clipping the edges of the side piece so that you can ease

it around the corners, and stitch. Pin the other edge of the side panel to the set aside lining back panel in the same way, clipping around the edges to ease the piece around the corners. Sew and turn right side out.

Slip the finished outer bag inside the lining so that wrong sides are together. Carefully slip stitch the lining in place by hand to secure. Turn the finished bag right side out.

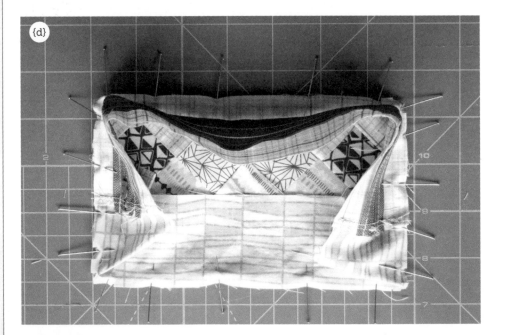

Patchwork Story

My connection to patchwork runs all the way back to my childhood when my grandmother pieced simple quilts together for each of her grandchildren. She had a handmade quilt frame that she'd stretch the finished piece across for tying, and I can still remember peeking over the edge of it to see what colors and patterns came together as she stitched her way across. Fast forward to today and I've found that I love being able to give these classic quilt pieces a modern update.

{07} Make the strap

To make the shoulder strap, cut two strips of light orange fabric and two strips of medium-weight fusible interfacing each measuring 24 x 2" (60 x 5.5 cm). Following the manufacturer's instructions, fuse each interfacing strip to the wrong side of each fabric strip. Stitch the strips together along one short edge to make one long strap. Turn under at each short edge by ¼" (6 mm) and press.

Fold the strap in half lengthwise with right sides together, and stitch along the length. Turn right side out and press flat, so that the seam lies in the middle of the back of the strap, then topstitch along each long edge to finish.

Take a metal hinge clip and loop the strap end onto it, overlapping the fabric by about 1" (2.5 cm). Connect the fabric loop securely to the strap by stitching a reinforced rectangle. Repeat to attach the other end of the strap to the second metal hinge clip the opposite side. Clip the metal hinge clips into the side loops on the bag to finish.

Foundation-pieced laundry bag

{ This roomy drawstring bag, inspired by vintage laundry bags of years gone by and decorated with a line of freshly washed clothes hanging out to dry, is a great place to keep those special garments that require hand washing. The "clothes" are made using foundation paper piecing, and a little hand embroidery is the perfect finishing touch.

MATERIALS

Small piece of pink novelty print fabric for the bra design

Red novelty print fabric 9 x 8" (23 x 20 cm) for the dress design

Blue gingham cotton fabric 4 x 6" (10 x 15 cm) for the skirt design center panel and waistband

¼ yard (0.25 meters) of 44–45" (112 cm) wide blue floral cotton fabric for the skirt design side panels and the drawstring channels for the bag

¾ yard (0.7 meters) of 44–45" (112 cm) wide red gingham cotton fabric for the bra design straps and the bag lining

1 yard (1 meter) of 44–45" (112 cm) wide linen fabric

3 yards (3 meters) of ½" (1.3 cm) wide red gingham ribbon

Coordinating cotton thread

Six-strand embroidery floss in the following colors: aqua, brown, yellow, black, and white

Lightweight copy paper or translucent vellum for foundation paper piecing

Water-soluble marker pen or pencil

SIZE
18 x 23½" (45 x 60 cm)

FEATURED TECHNIQUES
- Basic hand stitches: Decorative stitches (page 96)
- For more on foundation paper piecing, see page 102

CHARISE RANDELL

Charise Randell has been sewing since she was six, when she dreamed of becoming a fashion designer, and she grew up to do just that, working for companies including Nordstrom and Eddie Bauer. She designs patterns and writes for sewing magazines such as *Stitch Magazine* and *Sew News*. For links to her patterns and sewing tutorials visit www.ChariseCreates.blogspot.com.

BEFORE YOU BEGIN

For the very best results, read through the directions before starting. As you will want to launder the laundry bag often, be sure to prewash and press all fabric before use.

Use the templates on pages 156 and 157. If scanning and printing the foundation-pieced designs, set your printer to Page Scaling: None. Whether scanning and printing or enlarging and copying from a photocopier, do make sure that the test 1"/2.5 cm square provided measures accurately before cutting your fabrics.

All seams are ¼" (6 mm) unless otherwise stated. Do be sure to leave ¼" (6 mm) all around the individual sections that make up the paper-pieced bra, dress and skirt designs.

When paper piecing, reduce your stitch length to 1.5 mm (about 18 stitches per 1"/2.5 cm) as this will make it easier to remove the foundation backing paper.

Patchwork Story

My clothes-on-the-line laundry bag was inspired by the charm of vintage linens. There is nothing more enjoyable than being surrounded by beautiful handmade items that are used and admired every day. I designed this sweet laundry bag with just that in mind—a pretty place to keep your hand washables until wash day. It was made with lovely vintage-inspired Japanese fabrics and laundry-fresh linen.

METHOD

{01} Cut your fabrics for the bag

Cut the following pieces:
From the linen fabric:
One strip 10¾ x 1⅝" (27.3 x 4.1 cm) for left-hand border
One strip 10¾ x 2⅝" (27.3 x 6.7 cm) for right-hand border
One strip 4⅜ x 18¾" (11 x 47.5 cm) for top border
One strip 8⅛ x 18¾" (20.5 x 47.5 cm) for bottom border
One piece 18¾ x 22¼" (47.5cm x 56.5 cm) for backing

From the blue floral cotton fabric:
Two strips 5 x 18½" (13 x 47.5 cm) for the drawstring channels

From the red gingham cotton fabric:
Two pieces 18¾ x 22¼" (47.5 x 56.5 cm) for the lining

{02} Paper piece the skirt

a. Transfer the pattern template onto the paper or vellum. Cut the pattern template apart by letter unit (A and B). Following the photo of the completed skirt panel as your guide (page 76), cut your chosen fabric pieces making sure that they are at least ⅜" (1 cm) larger all around than the letter unit that they will be pieced over.

b. Working from the reverse (unprinted) side of letter unit A, place fabric right side up over section A1, making sure there is at least ⅜" (1 cm) around the perimeter of the pattern section. Pin the fabric to the pattern. (You may need to hold the pattern and fabric up to the light to correctly place the fabric on the pattern.)

c. Flip the pattern over to the printed side and fold the pattern back on the stitching line between A1 and A2. Trim ¼" (6 mm) beyond the line. This is your seam allowance.

d. Turn the pattern to the reverse side and place the second fabric piece A2 right sides together with A1, making sure once again that the fabric piece covering A2 is at least ⅜" (1 cm) larger than section A2. Pin in place.

e. Flip the pattern and fabric over to the printed side and stitch on the line between A1 and A2, starting the stitching where lines A1 and A2 intersect, backstitching at the beginning. Stitch beyond the pattern piece at the end of the stitching line.

f. Flip the pattern over and finger-press (see page 97).

g. Continue to add the fabric pieces in turn to unit A in numerical order, until the section is complete.

Paper piece letter unit B in the same way, working in numerical order and making sure to leave a ¼" (6 mm) seam allowance around each section.

Increase the stitch length to 2 mm (10–12 stitches per 1"/2.5 cm) and stitch unit A to B.

Note

Key to the success of the laundry bag foundation-pieced design is the careful selection of your printed fabrics, choosing prints at a scale that works for the garments. The red bow print fabric for the dress and the pink strawberry print for the bra are both designed by Atsuko Matsuyama for Yuwa Fabrics, and the sweet floral print used for the skirt is aptly named Flower Sugar from Lecien Fabrics.

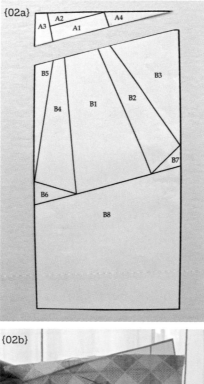

{02a}

{02b}

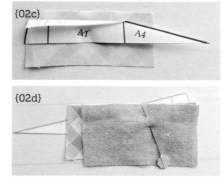

{02c}

{02d}

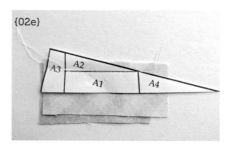

{02e}

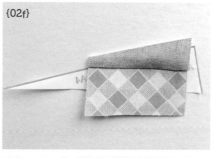

{02f}

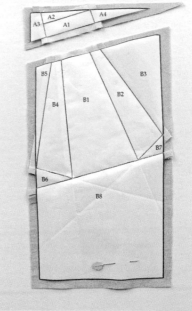

{02g}

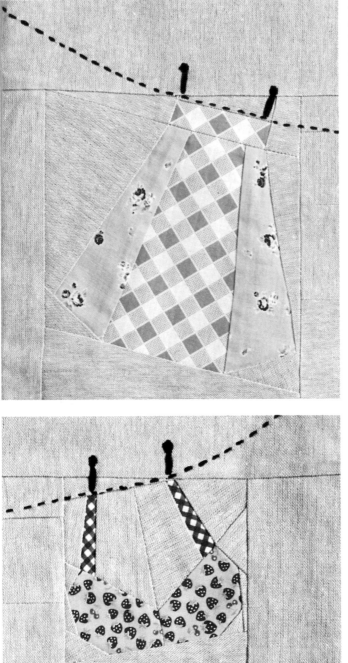

Detail from the completed skirt paper-pieced panel. Note: the paper piecing template is reversed.

Detail from the completed bra paper-pieced panel. Note: the paper piecing template is reversed.

{03} Paper piece the bra

a. Paper piece the bra, referring to step 2 for guidance, working to join each letter unit in numerical order. Cut the bra straps from the red gingham lining fabric, two pieces each measuring 2 x 3" (5 x 8 cm).

Use a 2mm stitch length (10–12 stitches per 1"/2.5 cm) and stitch unit A to D and unit B to C. Then stitch unit A/D to B/C. Attach section E to the top and F to the bottom, then attach section G to the bottom of the pieced block.

{03a}

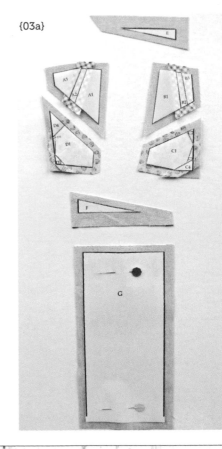

{04} Paper piece the dress

a. Paper piece the dress, referring to step 2 for guidance, working to join each letter unit in numerical order.

Use a 2mm stitch length (10–12 stitches per 1"/2.5 cm) and stitch unit A to B. Then stitch A/B to C and finally unit A/B/C to D.

Detail from the completed dress paper-pieced panel. Note: the paper piecing template is reversed.

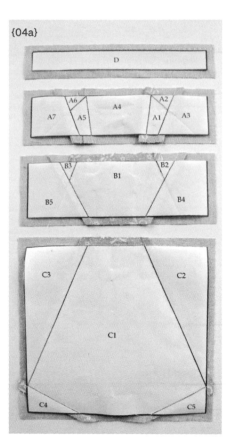

{04a}

{05} Assemble the bag front

Stitch the skirt unit to the dress unit, then the skirt/dress unit to the bra unit. Remove the pattern paper from the back of the pieced block.

Pin and sew the linen border pieces around the paper-pieced block in the following order and pressing seams as you go: left-hand side strip, right-hand side strip, top strip, bottom strip.

{06} Embroider the design

Transfer the bee embroidery pattern onto the bag front, just below the bra and to the right of the dress. To do this, make a copy of the bee template on page 156) and tape it to a window. Place the pieced fabric over the taped design and use a pencil to draw the outline of the bee onto the fabric. Continue to mark the bee flight across the bottom of the pieced panel freehand if you wish, following the photo on page 73 as your guide. Embroider the clothes line to align with the top of the paper-pieced garments using running stitch with stitches spaced about ⅛" (3 mm) apart and four strands of brown embroidery floss. Use two strands of brown embroidery floss to work the clothespins with satin stitch.

Embroider the bee: backstitch the outline (excluding wings) using two strands of black embroidery floss. Use satin stitch and two strands of black to fill in the head and two of the stripes, completing the remaining two stripes with two strands of yellow. Backstitch the wings using two strands of white embroidery floss. Embroider the bee's flight path using four strands of aqua embroidery floss and running stitches spaced ⅛" (3 mm) apart.

{07} Make and attach the channels for the drawstring

a. Take one of the blue floral drawstring channel strips and fold and press a double hem along both short sides. Fold over ¼" (6 mm) to the wrong side, press, fold over another ¼" (6 mm) and press again. Edge stitch close to the folded edge. Fold the strip in half lengthways, wrong sides facing, and press. Mark 1½" (4 cm) down from the folded edge and stitch along the marked line, back basting at the ends. Repeat for the other drawstring channel strip.

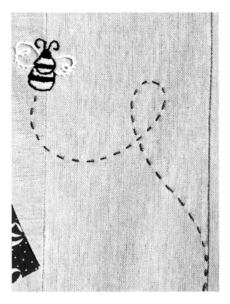

{07b}

b. Take one of the prepared drawstring channel strips and place with right sides facing along the center of the top of the front of the bag, matching the top raw edges and pin in place. Baste ⅜" (1 cm) from the raw edge. Repeat to attach the other drawstring channel strip to the bag backing piece.

{08} Assemble the bag

Place the front panel and the back panel right sides together, matching raw edges, and pin. Stitch around the sides and bottom of the bag with a ⅜" (1 cm) seam allowance, press seams open, and turn right side out.

Place your lining panels together with right sides facing and matching the raw edges. Pin along the sides and bottom, and stitch together with a ⅜" (1 cm) seam allowance, leaving a 3" (7.5 cm) opening on one side.

Place the outer bag inside the lining, so that right sides are together (the wrong side of the lining will be facing you). Match the top raw edges of the outer bag to the lining as well as the side seams. Pin in place and stitch around the top edge with a ⅜" (1 cm) seam allowance. Turn the bag right side out and press. To keep the lining in place, topstitch ⅜" (1 cm) down from the top edge of the linen. Slip stitch the opening in the lining closed by hand.

For the ribbon drawstrings, cut two lengths of the ribbon each 1½ yards (1.5 meters) long. Attach a safety pin to one edge of the ribbon, and use it to thread the ribbon through the drawstring channel on one side and back through the channel on the other side to come out where you began. Knot the ends. Working on the opposite side, thread the second ribbon length in the same way.

Choose a pretty gingham ribbon for the drawstrings to match your laundry bag's gingham fabric lining.

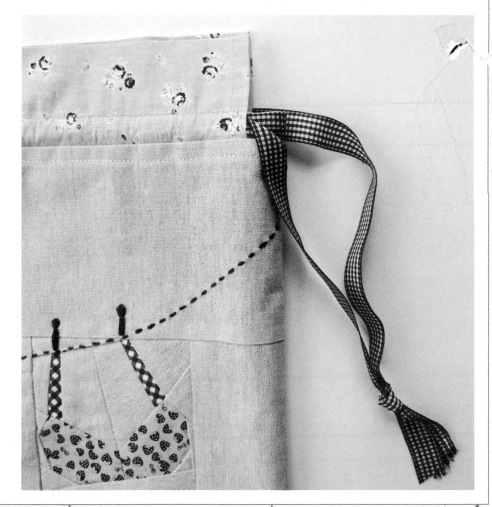

Drunkard's path flower placemats

{ Brighten up breakfast with this colorful set of placemats. The drunkard's path block is a great way to try out curved seams, and this new twist on a traditional design combines the quarter-circles with squares to create the rounded petal shapes of the flower design. It lends itself to using up your scraps, making these floral fancies both fun and functional.

MATERIALS (FOR FOUR PLACEMATS)

Scraps of solid and patterned cotton fabric at least 4 x 4" (10 x 10 cm) in yellow, red, blue, and orange shades

½ yard (0.5 meters) of 44–45" (112 cm) wide cotton fabric in neutral shade

1 yard (1 meter) of 44–45" (112 cm) wide coordinating cotton fabric for backing

¼ yard (0.25 meters) of 44–45" (112 cm) wide coordinating cotton fabric for binding

1 yard (1 meter) of 44–45" (112 cm) wide cotton batting cut into four equal-sized rectangles

Machine sewing thread to coordinate

Small plate for trimming corners

SIZE

Approx 17¼ x 15¾" (43.5 x 40 cm)

FEATURED TECHNIQUES

- Making templates (page 90)
- Machine piecing: Curved seams (page 99)
- Making a quilt sandwich (page 146)
- Continuous binding (page 152)
- For more on drunkard's path piecing and variations, see page 134

BEFORE YOU BEGIN

For our set, four different prints were used to bind the placemats, but you could use just one to create a coordinated look to the finished set.

Prewash and press fabrics before use as necessary: this is particularly important if you are using vintage fabrics as these may have dyes that run when washed.

Cut templates A and B on page 155 from card or plastic and use to cut out your fabrics.

When piecing the patchwork, pin and stitch together with right sides facing. **All seams are ¼" (6 mm).**

DESIGNED BY MALKA DUBRAWSKY

METHOD

{01} Cut your patchwork fabrics

Cut the following pieces:

From your scrap cotton fabric scraps:
12 pieces each in red, yellow, blue, and orange using template A
Four squares 3½ x 3½" (8.9 x 8.9 cm) each in red, yellow, blue, and orange

From the cotton in neutral shade:
48 pieces using template B
Eight rectangles 3¼ x 11¾" (8.3 x 29.8 cm) for border
Eight rectangles 17¼ x 2½" (44 x 6.3 cm) for border

{02} Piece the drunkard's path flower block

Note: Instructions are for making one placemat using the yellow shade fabrics; repeat to make the remaining three placemats in red, blue, and orange.

Fold one A piece and one B piece in half. Finger-press to mark midpoints. With right sides facing and aligning curved edges, pin A and B together at the outer edges, then join at the midpoints. Contine to pin together along the curve easing the pieces as you work (see photo top right).

Sew together and clip curves. Press seam to one side and open out. Repeat to make two more sewn quarters.

Pin two sewn quarters together, sew and press seam open. Pin the remaining sewn quarter to the fabric scrap square. Sew together and press seam open.

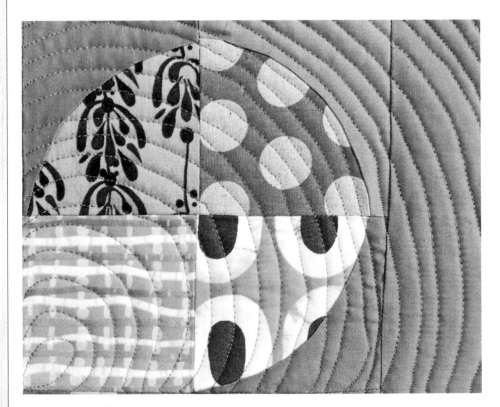

Patchwork Story

I've long loved drunkard's path, but when I discovered that I could make the pattern into a flower-like shape by adding a square block to the mix, I had a real "Aha!" moment. I do a lot of piecing, but almost no appliqué work, so it's rare that I make a block that feels representational. I loved the opportunity this gave me to create something that was very shape-oriented and therefore, very familiar—I feel like I got to draw and design at the same time. What a treat.

Pin the joined pairs and stitch together to complete the piecing of the first flower petal section. Press seam open. Using a clear, acrylic quilter's rule, trim the excess (about ¼"/6 mm) along the sides of the non-petal square.

Make three more flower petal sections. Take two flower petal sections and pin together so that edges with non-petal squares are aligned. Sew and press seam open. Repeat with remaining flower petal sections. Pin the joined pairs, together, making sure that the non-petal squares are in the center of the flower. Sew and press seam open. The flower block is complete.

{03} Add borders to pieced block

Pin one 3¼ x 11¾" (8.3 x 29.8 cm) rectangle to one edge of the pieced flower block. Sew together and press seam open. Repeat to join the second 3¼ x 11¾" (8.3 x 29.8 cm) rectangle to the opposite edge. Pin and sew a 17¼ x 2½" (44 x 6.3 cm) rectangle in turn to the remaining edges of the pieced flower block, pressing seams open each time.

{04} Make quilt sandwich and quilt

From your backing fabric, cut a rectangle a little larger than the pieced top. Working on a clean flat surface, layer up your quilt sandwich with the backing piece wrong side facing up, batting in the middle, and patchwork on top, right side facing up. Using your preferred method (see page 146), fix the layers together. Machine quilt, removing basting as you work. The placemats shown were echo quilted, starting from the center and working outward following the floral motif of the piecing. Once the quilting is complete, trim layers flush.

Mark the rounded corners with a small plate and trim (or use a rotary cutter to trim directly around the edge of the plate). Clip the curves.

{05} Bind and finish the placemat

Cut your binding fabric into 1½" (4 cm) strips and join to make one long strip. Cut off a strip from the joined strip long enough to bind one placemat. Bind using the continuous binding technique for single binding, but easing the binding around the rounded corners. Turn under a ¼" (6 mm) seam allowance, pin binding to reverse of placemat, and slip stitch in place.

Make and bind the other three placemats in the same way.

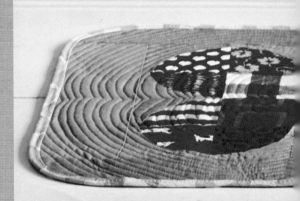

New to patchwork?

This section of the book contains all the step-by-step guidance you need to get started. So choose your fabric, grab your scissors, and read on—in just a short while you'll be patchwork perfect!

Seasoned pro?

If you've already completed a few patchwork projects, use this section to build up your skills. Packed with hints, tips, and techniques, it will encourage you to explore variations on some of the most popular patchwork blocks, and there are even some templates provided to help you to practice making your designs (see Exploring Patchwork, page 153).

Techniques

Tools and materials

> The good news is that for patchwork you really don't need much specialized equipment—in fact for many centuries the most beautiful pieces of work have been created just with fabric, scissors, needle and thread! However, if there is a gadget on the market that is going to save you time, why wouldn't you use it? Consider your options.

MARKING AND MEASURING TOOLS

You probably have perfectly adequate tools for measuring and marking in your sewing box or on your desk, but a few special purchases could make your life a little easier when making your patchwork projects.

MARKING TOOLS

Test the marker on a spare piece of fabric first to see if it will show up, and also to find out whether the marks can be removed easily.

Disappearing marker pen: There are various types—water-soluble (use on washable fabrics only), air-soluble (marks will fade over time), and pens where the lines disappear when iron-heat is applied.

Chalk pencil/tailor's pencil: These often have a stiff brush at one end for removing the chalk marks.

Lead pencil: Useful for drawing out pattern templates, but not ideal for fabric unless used on the wrong side.

Tailor's chalk: Available in a range of colors, marks can be brushed away easily when no longer needed.

Chalk wheel: An up-to-date version of tailor's chalk, filled with chalk dust.

MEASURING TOOLS

For patchwork piecing, accurate measuring is vitally important for good results. Use the right tools and take your time at this stage to prevent problems later.

Acrylic quilter's rule: See Cutting Tools: Quilter's Rule, opposite.

Metal ruler: Best for making a cut when you need to draw a craft knife along a straight edge.

Tape measure: Avoid fabric tapes, as these can stretch over time.

Compass: For drawing out straight-forward circles and simple curves.

Seam gauge: A useful piece of equipment to produce seams of an even depth—also good for measuring borders accurately.

Quilter's quarter: A length of acrylic that can be used to add a perfect ¼" (6 mm) seam allowance around any straight-sided template.

Note

If you would like to have a go at designing your own patchwork block designs there are a couple of extras that could prove useful. A T-square comes in handy for achieving right-angled corners, and an adjustable set square (available in a range of sizes) is ideal for measuring and marking lines at a wide range of angles.

CUTTING AND SEWING TOOLS

Good cutting is as important as measuring as far as patchwork is concerned so make sure you have the best tools for the job. A standard sewing machine is all you need to make the projects in this book, but if you plan to invest in a new sewing machine and think you might make patchwork quilts regularly, here is some advice on what to look for.

CUTTING TOOLS

Although you can manage with just a sharp pair of good scissors, there is other equipment available that will speed up the cutting process considerably—as well as ensuring that the cuts you make are more accurate.

Fabric scissors: These should be very sharp with long blades. Generally, avoid using fabric scissors to cut anything but fabric, as they will soon become blunt.

Rotary cutter: This will cut through several layers of fabric in one go, making it much easier to cut accurate shapes for patchwork. They are available with straight or curved handles, so try out several different sorts to find the one that suits you best. Rotary cutters are generally used together with a quilter's rule and cutting mat.

Quilter's rule: Specially made rulers that make measuring and cutting fabrics for patchwork altogether quicker. The markings are available in different colors, so choose one that is clear against your cutting mat.

Self-healing cutting mat: This provides a good cutting surface and protects your work surface when you are using a rotary cutter. Usually one side is marked with a grid and the other is plain. The grid is handy for lining up fabric and ruler, but don't use it as a measure. To keep mats from buckling, store them flat or hang them up and out of direct sunlight.

Craft knife: Ideal for cutting template plastic and cardboard.

SEWING TOOLS

Hand sewing needles: "Sharps" (ordinary sewing needles) for general sewing and piecing, "betweens" for hand quilting, and embroidery needles for decorative stitching.

Pins: While any type of pin is suitable, you can buy special quilter's pins that are longer than normal in order to go through several layers of fabric. Choose easy-to-see pins with large colored heads. Never machine stitch over pins, but remove them as you go.

Thread scissors: A small pair of scissors with sharp points is ideal for snipping thread and for fine-detail fabric cutting.

Seam ripper: If your patchwork units end up a little smaller or larger than each other, this will prove invaluable to take a section apart and fix it.

Sewing machine: A machine with an extension table that can be attached to the side of it is useful to support large patchwork quilt projects, and the larger the throat space between the needle housing and the other side of the machine, the easier it will be to machine-quilt large quilts.

Investing in a few key tools, such as a rotary cutter, a self-healing cutting mat and quilter's rules, for example, can really speed things up.

Useful sewing machine feet

Walking foot: When sewing several layers of fabric, a walking foot makes sure that the top and bottom layers of fabric are pulled along at the same speed for a smooth stitching line, and prevents puckering.

Quarter-inch foot: This measures exactly ¼" (6 mm) from the point of the needle to the inner edge of the foot, to allow you to sew a seam allowance quickly and accurately. It may have a guide on it to prevent the fabric from going past the edge. It is sometimes known as a "little foot."

Appliqué foot: A clear, hinged foot that allows the sewing underneath to remain clearly visible. It is easy to maneuver when sewing appliquéd pieces.

Ditch quilting foot: A foot with an extended guide that helps you to remain in the seam while the machine stitches.

TOOLS FOR TEMPLATE CUTTING

Manufactured patchwork templates may seem expensive, but they offer a high degree of accuracy. Alternatively, you can make your own with a few essential materials.

Ready-made patchwork templates: Choose either a double unit—with one solid piece for backing papers and marking seam allowances, and one piece with a cut-out window so you can view motif positioning— or a multi-sized unit with ¼" (6 mm) gradations.

Template plastic and cardboard: For making your own templates and stencils. While cardboard is adequate for single usage, you should choose plastic for multiple usage as it will hold its shape better.

Tracing paper: Essential for copying and transferring shapes to paper, cardboard or fabric, or for creating your own designs and motifs.

Squared or isometric graph paper: Handy for templates, planning out a design, or when working out different block setting patterns.

Freezer paper: Coated with plastic on one side so it can be ironed on fabric and later removed without leaving a trace, this is ideal for appliqué templates and English paper piecing.

A see-through plastic template is essential for fussy cutting, a technique used for the center motif and blades of the Dresden plate tea cozy. Simply align the template on the fabric so a desired element (usually a motif) is in the center area of the template.

Paper scissors: Cutting paper patterns and templates can blunt scissor blades, so never use paper scissors to cut fabric. They can be used to cut synthetic batting though.

OTHER ESSENTIAL EQUIPMENT

Iron and ironing board: For removing creases from your fabrics before beginning work, and to press seams while piecing.

Sticky notes: These are a good way to keep track of the order of your fabric units prior to stitching them together into pieced blocks.

Temporary basting spray: This can be used to hold fabric layers together temporarily, when quilting for example.

Safety pins: These can also be used to hold the layers of a quilt together while quilting—safety pins are so much more secure than using straight pins.

Thread: Choose an ordinary sewing thread to match the fabric (cotton for pure cotton, polyester for polycotton) when piecing. It can also be used for quilting; however, special pre-waxed quilting thread is stronger and is available in a wide range of colors.

Thimble: When quilting by hand, this will prevent pricked fingers.

Embroidery floss: Useful for tied quilting or for appliqué embellishment. It is stranded, so you can use one or more strands.

FABRICS

If you are a beginner, the best type of fabric to use for patchwork is 100% cotton fabric. It is very easy to fold, presses well, feels good to handle as you work, and can be washed without any problems.

CHOOSING AND USING FABRIC

There are a huge amount of plain colors (also known as solids) and printed patterns to choose from. In general, small-scale patterns work best, particularly when piecing. Quilting will show up less well on patterned fabric than on plain, so keep the quilting simple on patterned blocks.

When using patterned fabric to make small squares or geometric shapes, you must cut very accurately (particularly a repetitive geometric pattern, such as little dots or flowers)—if you go slightly askew it will be very obvious. Make sure you cut all patterned pieces the same way up.

When combining different prints, try to follow a theme or the quilt may start to look uncoordinated. For instance, you may choose to use lots of different prints and plains in the same basic color; here the color is the coordinating factor. Or you may choose lots of multicolored fabrics that all have one or two colors in common, or are all a similar color value. If you find choosing difficult, a good way to start is to buy ready-selected fabric packs, which have been combined to work well together (see below).

Unless working with pre-cut fabric bundles, which do not require prewashing, wash each fabric color separately in hot water to pre-shrink, then press while still damp for a smooth, crease-free finish. Discard any fabrics that bleed.

Pre-cut fabric bundles

Fat quarters: This is about a quarter of a yard. Instead of being cut in a narrow strip across the full width of the fabric, the yard is cut in half down its length and then each half is cut in half again across the width to give four oblongs of fabric usually around 18 x 22" (45 x 55 cm). Fat eighths, measuring about 9 x 22" (23 x 55 cm) are also available.

Layer cakes™: Collections of fabric squares measuring about 10 x 10" (25 x 25 cm).

Charm packs: Collections of fabric squares measuring about 5 x 5" (13 x 13 cm). Mini charm packs (about 2½ x 2½"/ 6.5 x 6.5 cm) are also available.

Jelly rolls™: Strips of fabric cut about 2½" (6.5 cm) wide by the width of the fabric.

BATTING

This forms the middle layer of a patchwork quilt and its original purpose was to make the quilt warm. Old quilts often feature worn-out blankets or otherwise unusable fabric as a layer of batting. These days, manufactured batting is sold by length from a roll or in standard cut sizes.

TYPES OF BATTING

In general, batting is white, but it is also available in dark gray and black. There are several choices.

Polyester batting: Lightweight, inexpensive, and available in many lofts (thicknesses), this type of batting does not shrink, can be machine-washed, and is quick to dry.

Cotton batting: Ideal for small projects and fairly easy to work, if a little dense. It should be prewashed as it will shrink, which can cause the quilt to pucker after washing.

Wool batting: This is significantly thinner than other types, but retains its loft well. Check cleaning instructions as it may not be washable.

Fusible batting: This is good for small projects as it eliminates the need for basting, and there is no need to prewash it.

Batting loft: Thin, lightweight batting ideal for quilts that will be used as wall hangings or displayed in other ways.

Basic techniques

{ *In this chapter you will find all the basic techniques required to get started with patchwork, from making templates and using a rotary cutter, to essential methods for hand and machine piecing. With info on basic stitches and pressing too, you'll be patchwork perfect in no time.*

USING TEMPLATES TO CUT SHAPES

Accuracy is crucial when cutting out shapes for patchwork, particularly when making a series of identical blocks. Templates and paper patterns will help make the process of cutting many shapes much easier.

Note

A block is a term used for a single patchwork unit, usually square, which can be joined together with many others to make up the top of a quilt.

MAKING TEMPLATES

Templates can be made in paper, card or template plastic. If you only want to use a template a couple of times, paper or card will be quite adequate.

Note

Always use a craft knife and a metal ruler to cut cardboard and template plastic—plastic rulers are easily damaged. Make sure the blade is really sharp to avoid rough edges on the template. If you are cutting several templates, change the blade as soon as it becomes harder to cut—this is a sign that the blade is becoming blunt.

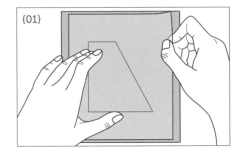
{01}

To cut a quantity of irregular shapes, first make a template. Draw around the shape on tracing paper, then either transfer the line to a piece of card or glue the tracing paper to the card.

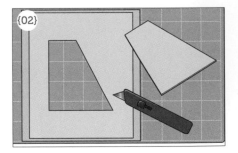
{02}

Cut out the shape, following the line very carefully. If you are not cutting many shapes, you can use this cardboard template. For cutting a large number of shapes, however, it is safer to use a template made of special template plastic.

PAPER PATTERNS

If the shape has curved lines or is complex, a paper pattern may be easier to use. Invest in some very thin paper—special pattern paper can be bought but a lightweight printing paper will work just as well.

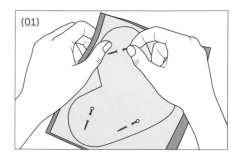

{01}

Trace the shape onto thin, lightweight paper, then pin the paper to the fabric. It will be easier to cut along the marked line if you don't cut out the paper shape before pinning. Cut along the line, through paper and fabric.

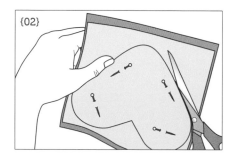

{02}

You can probably cut several pieces at the same time, as long as the shape is not very complex or the fabric very thick. Use sharp fabric scissors, but it is important to use thin, lightweight paper to avoid blunting your scissors.

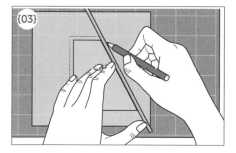

{03}

Draw around the shape to transfer it to a piece of template plastic. If you are making a window template, add a ¼" (6 mm) border on all sides for the seam allowance. You can either measure this by hand or use a quilter's quarter (page 86).

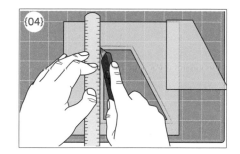

{04}

Cut out the inner window. Then cut around the seam allowance line. The inner window is for support papers or for marking the stitching line. The outside of the template is for cutting fabric patches accurately.

WINDOW TEMPLATES

Window templates are ideal to cut the papers for English paper piecing (see page 94).

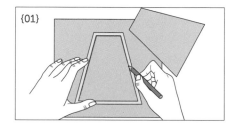

{01}

Use the inside window of the template to mark the backing paper. Cut one paper for each fabric piece.

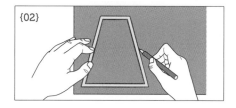

{02}

Use the outside edge of the template to cut the fabric pieces. If possible, align the template with the straight grain and don't drag the marker as this may stretch the fabric out of shape.

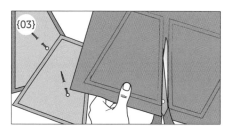

{03}

Cut out the fabric and paper pieces. Pin a paper piece to the wrong side of each fabric piece.

ROTARY CUTTING

Rotary cutting can make the cutting process much faster as it allows you to cut through several fabric layers in one go to create many identical shapes. Rotary cutting equipment is also invaluable for measuring fabrics and pieced units, and checking that they are square and right-angled. Rotary-cut strips can be stitched together in sequence and then cut across into pieced strips, which can be assembled in a different way.

Note

When working with a rotary cutter, take great care to follow safety guidelines. There are many different brands of cutter, so find the one that best suits you. A rotary cutter has an extremely sharp blade, so it comes with a safety guard. Make sure you put the guard back on the blade as soon as you finish cutting, to prevent any accidents. Always cut away from yourself, and replace dull or damaged blades as soon as you notice them. A self-healing cutting mat will protect the work surface and extend the life of the cutting blades.

USING A ROTARY CUTTER

To avoid cutting by mistake into the section of fabric you actually want to use, cover it with the rotary ruler and cut away the waste.

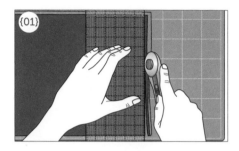

Fold the fabric along the straight grain and fit it on to the mat. Align the folded edge along one of the mat lines, then use the rotary ruler to straighten the raw edge.

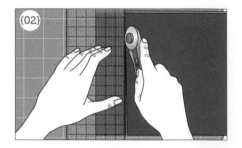

Turn the piece of fabric around and measure the width of the piece you want to cut. Cover the measured piece with the rotary ruler. Cut carefully along the grain.

CUTTING PIECED STRIPS

After you have made up pieced units, you may need to cut them into smaller units to stitch together in a different orientation to create the block design.

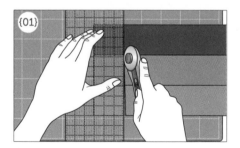

First stitch the strips together in the order you need. Press the seams to one side. Lay the pieced fabric right side up, trim the edge and then measure and place one of the grid lines of the ruler along the trimmed edge. Cut a series of pieced strips to the size required.

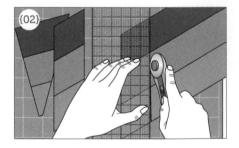

If you want to cut the pieced strips at an angle, measure the angle and trim off the edge. Then align the ruler on the trimmed edge and cut the pieced strips as in step 1.

HAND PIECING

Piecing by hand is often much quicker and easier than working on a machine—particularly if you are working with very small pieces, curved seams, or seams that are cut on the bias. You may find hand stitching much more relaxing and meditative than working on a machine, and there is the added advantage that you can carry bits of your project about with you to work on when you have a spare moment.

SINGLE STRAIGHT SEAMS

Stitching a perfectly straight seam may require a bit of practice. Starting and stopping on the seam line is the key to accurate piecing at corners. Small pieces can be joined together with a small, neat running stitch or backstitch (see Basic Hand Stitches, page 95).

{01}

{02}

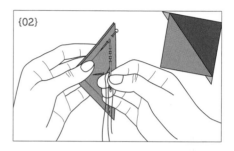

Lay the two pieces with right sides together, matching raw edges and corners. Pin the two pieces firmly in place.

Sew along the seam line, making sure that you start and finish exactly in the corner so there will be no gap at these points. Press the seam toward the darker fabric (see Pressing, page 97).

JOINING SEAMED PIECES

When you want to join a pair of seamed units, it is better to stitch outward from the seam in the center, so it will stay aligned across both units.

{01}

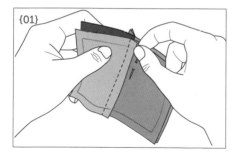

{02}

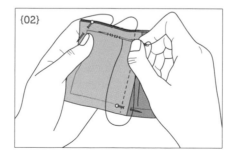

{03}

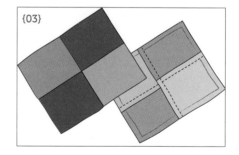

Join two pairs of pieces together, as described for single straight seams. Pin the two units together, right sides facing, matching the seams exactly.

Stitch the units together, working one side from the center outward along the seam line, then sewing the other side in the same way.

Press the seams flat on the wrong side. On the right side (seen above left) the four sides should line up perfectly in the middle.

ENGLISH PAPER PIECING

This is a traditional method of hand piecing using paper templates inside the block elements to guide where the edges are turned under. The paper templates remain inside the fabric pieces until they are all stitched together, and then they are removed.

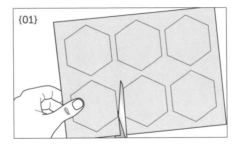

{01}

Make a plastic window template (see page 91). Use the inside window to mark the shape on paper—you will need one paper template for each piece. Iron the fabric, then use the outer edge of the template to mark the fabric shapes. Cut out the paper and fabric shapes.

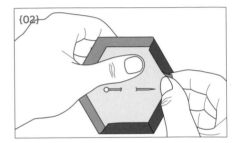

{02}

Center a paper template on the wrong side of one of the fabric pieces, making sure the seam allowance is the same all the way round, then pin in place. Fold the edges of the fabric over the paper, making sure the corners are neatly tucked in. Baste around the shape to attach the fabric to the paper. Repeat with the other pieces.

Note

When you stitch your hexagons around the template in step 2, instead of basting through the paper template you could stitch *only* through the fabric and take two little stitches at each point. By not stitching through the paper template, you won't have any basting stitches to remove at the end and the template will be easy to remove and can be used again.

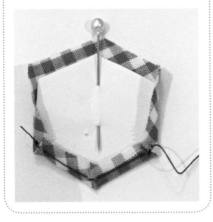

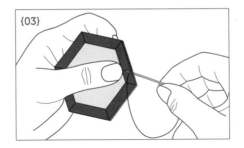

{03}

Place two pieces with right sides together, aligning the edges and corners. Whipstitch along each edge to hold the two pieces together, being very careful not to stitch through the paper template. Keep adding pieces in the same way to make up the design.

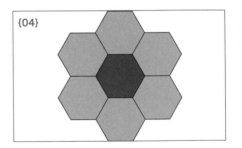

{04}

Leave the paper templates in place until all the pieces of a unit have been joined. As you make up each unit, press it flat. If making a quilt top, join up the units in the same way, removing the paper patterns before you add batting and backing.

BASIC HAND STITCHES

There are some hand stitches that you will use time and again in many different situations when making up your patchwork projects and piecing the patchwork itself. In some cases it is much easier and quicker to hand stitch pieces together than to use a machine.

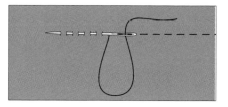

RUNNING STITCH

Used to join flat layers of fabric, or as a decoration. Take the needle in and out of the fabric several times, making a small stitch each time to create a row of even and evenly spaced stitches. Pull the thread through gently until it is taut, but not too tight, then continue stitching as before.

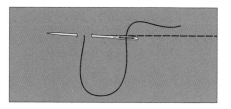

BACKSTITCH

Used to join flat layers of fabric in a secure way, or as a decoration. From the front the stitches run end to end like machine stitching. Bring the needle through the fabric to the right side, then insert it a short distance behind where it came out and bring it up through the fabric the same distance ahead. Each subsequent stitch begins at the end of the previous stitch and the needle comes up again an equal distance ahead, so the stitches are the same size.

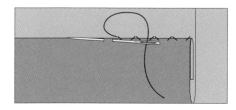

SLIP STITCH

Used to join two folded edges together, or a folded edge to a flat piece, so that the stitches are almost invisible. Bring the needle up through the folded edge of one side, take a tiny stitch through just one or two threads in the opposite layer or fold, then insert the needle back into the fold of the first layer. Slide the needle along inside the fold a short way, then repeat the sequence.

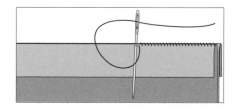

WHIPSTITCH

Another stitch used to join two folded edges, also called oversewing or overcasting. Insert the needle at a slight angle through the edges of both folds, picking up one or two threads on each edge. Pull the thread all the way through, then repeat the stitch. Whipstitch is usually worked from left to right, but can be worked the other way if it feels more comfortable, as long as you are consistent.

BASTING

Basting is a temporary method of holding layers of fabric together until they are stitched permanently together, either with a seam or by quilting. It is worked like running stitch but with longer stitches.

Note

When hand stitching, start with a length of thread about 24" (60 cm) long—if any longer it may tangle after being pulled through the fabric a few times. Always buy good-quality thread as cheap thread breaks easily.

DECORATIVE STITCHES

There are several stitches that you will need for embellishing your projects, including French knots and satin stitch shown here, and backstitch and running stitch worked decoratively, (see page 96).

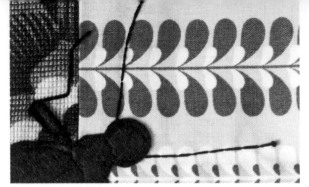

French knots finish off the top of each backstitched antennas on the beetle appliqués that scuttle across the nine-patch beanbag (pages 9–13).

FRENCH KNOTS

A decorative stitch, this is a compact raised stitch resembling a bead lying on its side, often used for details such as eyes on an appliqué motif.

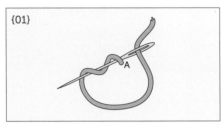

{01}

Come up at A and wrap thread around needle twice in a counter-clockwise direction.

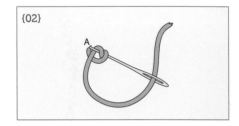

{02}

Push wraps together and slide to end of needle. Take needle back down close to start point, pulling thread through to form knot.

SATIN STITCH

This stitch is made up of simple straight stitches laid close together in parallel lines to create a solid, smooth filling stitch ideal for filling in motifs.

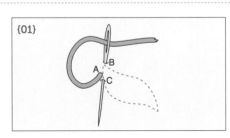

{01}

Come up at A, go down at B, and come up at C. Pull thread through gently ready for next stitch.

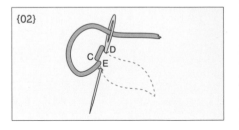

{02}

Placing stitches close together, go down at D and come up at E. Follow exact guidelines of motif for even edge.

The bee embroidery on the foundation-pieced laundry bag (pages 72–79) is outlined with backstitch then filled in with satin stitch. The bee's flight path is worked with a decorative running stitch.

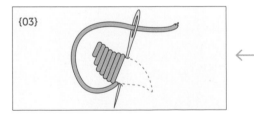

{03}

← Continue to fill your motif keeping an even tension so that the surface remains smooth.

PRESSING

The pressing of seams and blocks as you work is a basic part of any patchwork project. But remember "press" means just that: use the weight and heat of the iron. Don't drag the iron along a seam, particularly if the fabric has been cut on the bias, as you may stretch the piece out of shape.

Note

Piecing accuracy is improved by pressing each quilt unit or block as you make it, to ensure they fit together as they should. Unpressed seams have a tiny amount of fabric caught up, and this tiny amount can add up over many blocks, making the block smaller than it should be. If blocks vary in design and number of seams, you will end up with inaccurate sizes and blocks that don't match their neighbors.

FINGER-PRESSING

Some short seams can be finger pressed to save time. With the seam facing upward, press down the seam allowance with your finger or thumb so that it lies flat. For a slightly sharper crease, run the edge of your fingernail down the seam line but be careful not to stretch the fabric.

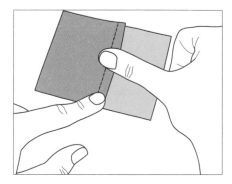

PRESSING WITH AN IRON

Always press your fabrics before measuring and cutting, to remove creases that would affect accuracy. Long or intricate seams are easier to press with an iron, and a patchwork project should also be carefully pressed before it is quilted. Set the iron to the correct temperature for the fabric and threads you are using. Seams are generally pressed toward the darker fabric, to avoid creating shadows on pale fabric on the front of the work, but you can also press them open. Press the seam as sewn first, to set the stitches. Now, with

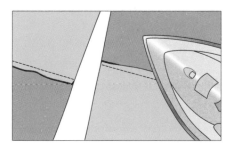

the seam facing up, press down with the iron until the seam allowance lies flat (either to one side or open as preferred). When joining units or rows of blocks, press seams in opposite directions when you can, so the seams "lock" or "nest" together when you sew units together.

Note

If you use fusible webbing or interfacing, make sure you don't get adhesive on the sole plate of the iron—use a pressing cloth or a sole plate cover. Be aware of the fabric type before you iron it. Durable fabrics, such as cotton, can take a fairly high temperature, which will make the task much easier. However, heat can damage delicate fabrics, so use a lower temperature when ironing synthetic fabrics or blends. Use a pressing cloth on synthetics and wool to avoid marking them.

MACHINE PIECING

A simple sewing machine is all that is required for most patchwork projects, but there are also machines that are specifically designed to meet the requirements of quilters so this might be something to consider if you are investing in a new machine. For more advice, see page 87 and page 88.

STRIPS

A straight seam and an accurate seam allowance are both essential if you want to achieve perfectly aligned strips.

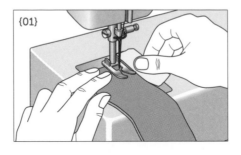
{01}

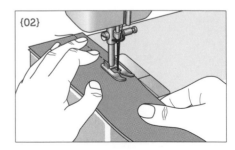
{02}

A special foot that measures an exact ¼" (6 mm) seam allowance is available for most machines, but marking the needle plate with a strip of masking tape is just as effective. Check the measurement on a scrap piece of fabric before you begin sewing a new project and replace the tape if it becomes worn or grubby.

Cut a good selection of strips to work with. Take two and place them with right sides together, lining up the raw edges. Stitch the two pieces together, taking care to keep the seam straight and at exactly ¼" (6 mm) from the raw edges.

CHAIN PIECING

You can speed up the process of making a block or quilt by chain piecing as much as possible.

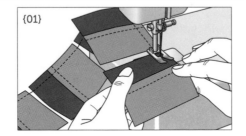
{01}

{02}

Cut a good selection of each of the various pieces you will be using and place them in separate piles near your machine. Feed one unit after another through the machine, stitching continuously without pausing to raise the presser foot or cut the thread between units.

You will end up with a chain of units, held together by a short length of thread. Cut the units apart when you have finished stitching.

CURVED SEAMS

When working on curved seams, be very careful not to stretch the fabric out of shape, or the finished unit will not lie flat when pressed.

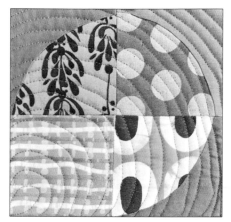

The curved seams of the quarter-circles when combined with a square create the rounded petal shapes on the drunkard's path flower placemats (pages 80–83).

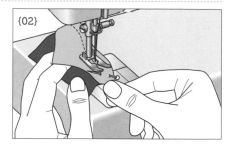

{01}

Working on the wrong side, mark the stitching line on one piece. Align the two pieces to be stitched together with right sides facing. Pin at right angles to the stitching line.

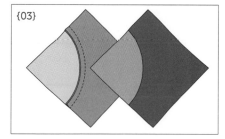

{03}

{02}

Place the unit under the needle and lower the needle at the end of the marked stitching line. Lower the presser foot and stitch slowly along the line, removing pins as you go.

← Clip the curve if necessary, then press the seam toward the concave edge.

JOINING PIECED UNITS

The biggest problem when joining many pieced units is getting all the seams to line up correctly. Make sure you join pieces together in the correct order, and keep checking their alignment as you work.

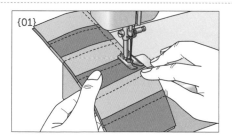

{01}

Make up a selection of pieced units and press the seams to one side. Place two units with right sides together, aligning raw edges and matching seams. Stitch the units together.

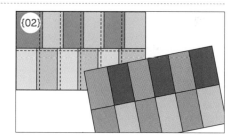

{02}

Press the seams to one side on the reverse (shown above left). On the right side (above right), the seam lines between the pieces should run in a perfectly straight line, with perfectly square corners.

JOINING PLAIN AND PIECED UNITS

When joining a pieced square to a plain square, the stitched point of the triangle should fall exactly on the seam allowance.

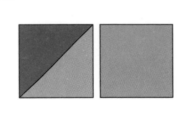

{01}

When joining a pieced unit and a plain unit, make sure they are the same size before sewing together.

{02}

Place the pieced unit and the plain unit with right sides together and stitch. On the right side, the diagonal seam on the pieced unit should fall exactly ¼" (6 mm) below the edge of the block, to act as a seam allowance when the units are sewn together with another unit.

TRIANGLE SQUARES

Triangle squares are the basis for several traditional block designs. These units are often called half-square triangles and there are many different ways to make them. Perhaps the easiest way is to take two squares of different colors and cut them in half along the diagonal to make four triangles. Place two contrasting triangles together with raw edges on the diagonal aligned and corners matching. Stitch the triangles together, being careful not to stretch the fabric. Open the unit and press the seams toward the darker fabric. A faster method, which makes two units at once, is described here.

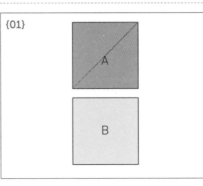

{01}

A

B

For each block cut one square each of fabrics A and B. Mark a diagonal line on the wrong side of square A, being careful not to stretch the fabric on the bias.

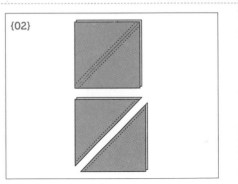

{02}

With right sides together, place square A on top of square B, with the diagonal line showing. Stitch ¼" (6 mm) away from the line down one side, then turn and sew back ¼" (6 mm) away down the other side. Cut along the diagonal line between the two lines of stitching.

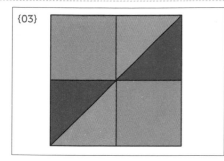

{03}

When the paired units are stitched to the next pair, all of the corners should meet exactly in the center. To achieve this, accurate measuring and stitching of seams is absolutely essential.

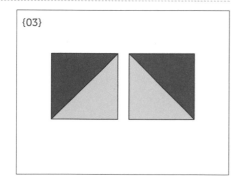

{03}

Press the triangle squares flat, with the seams toward the darker side. You now have two identical units.

A total of 144 triangle squares are required to make the design for the oversized broken dishes floor cushion (pages 34–39).

FOUNDATION PAPER PIECING

In this technique, pieces are stitched in order on to a foundation (or backing) fabric. It is ideal for irregular shapes and edges cut on the bias, as the foundation fabric will stabilize them.

Draw the pattern of the block on the foundation fabric, which can be a non-woven stabilizer or a suitable fabric or paper. Number the shapes in the order that they have to be stitched, working from the center outward.

Trace the pattern of the block on to tracing paper and cut this into the individual pieces. Use these as templates to cut the pieces of fabric. Remember to add a ¼" (6 mm) seam allowance all around the edge of each.

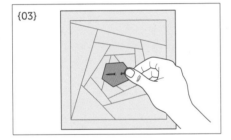

Place the foundation fabric on the work surface, with the unmarked side facing up. Place the first piece of fabric on top, in its relevant position, and pin in place. Check on the reverse to make sure the fabric piece covers the stitching line all round.

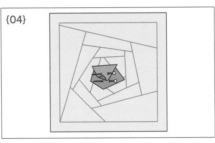

Place the second piece of fabric on top of the first piece (right sides together) with edges aligned so that when it flips over, it will be in its correct position in the design. Pin in place.

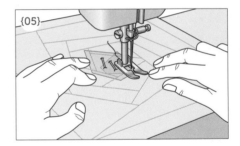

Working with the marked side of the foundation fabric facing you, stitch the marked line between the first two shapes. Turn over, flip the second piece of fabric into its correct position and press.

Note

Non-woven stabilizer is a fabric made by bonding fibers with adhesive or by needle-punching with a serrated needle so friction causes the fibers to cling together. It is not particularly strong, but as it does not stretch, it is ideal as a stable foundation fabric.

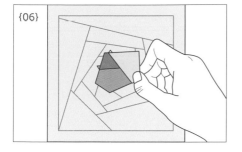

{06}

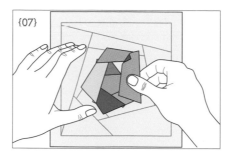

{07}

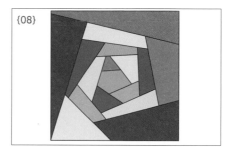

{08}

Place the third piece of fabric on top of the other two (right sides together) with edges aligned, so that when it flips over it will be in its correct position in the design. Pin in place, then sew.

Continue to sew on the pieces, keeping carefully to the marked order on the foundation fabric.

When the block is complete, press, and trim the edges to square it up as necessary.

Foundation paper piecing can seem complicated, as you stitch from the back of the work, but it is invaluable for piecing irregular shapes, such as those used to create the clothes on the laundry bag (pages 72–79). Just make sure your cut pieces cover and overlap the shape, and then stitch carefully along the marked lines.

Note

If you are foundation piecing an unsymmetrical design, remember that the pattern on the final block will be a mirror image of the original drawn pattern when it is finished. This is because you stitch the fabric pieces to the reverse of the foundation fabric—the unmarked side—so you can see the stitching lines and follow them to sew the fabric in place. You therefore need to place the templates for the fabric pieces the right way up on the wrong side of the fabric, so the pieces will be correct and not back to front.

Piecing with strips

Strips are the simplest shapes that can be pieced together, but despite this there is a very wide range of interesting designs that can be achieved with them. One of the best-known strip-based blocks is log cabin (see page 107), but there are plenty more featured in this section for you to try out.

RAIL FENCE

For rail fence at least three different fabrics are first strip-pieced, then cut into squares. The squares are rotated and alternated to create a zigzag pattern across the block, which can be made as a four- or nine-patch. Blocks can be set to create secondary patterns across a quilt.

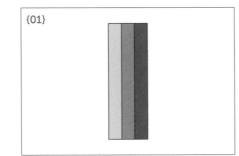

{01}

Cut strips in fabrics A, B and C, all of an equal width. Stitch them together along the long edge, using a ¼" (6 mm) seam. Press the seams to one side. Cut the pieced strips into several equal-sized squares.

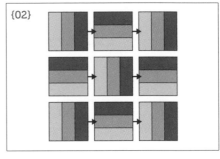

{02}

Alternate the striped squares horizontally and vertically. Stitch them together into three rows, as indicated in the diagram. Press the seams in alternate directions.

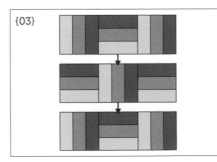

{03}

Join the three rows to form a block. For a professional-looking result, be very careful that seams match perfectly across the rows. Press the seams in opposite directions where possible, which will help the block to lie flat.

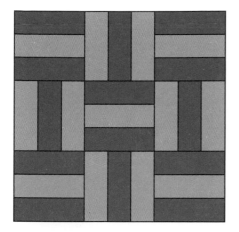

BASKETWEAVE

This block is made up of only two different fabrics, placed alternately. When the pieced squares are alternated and joined in exactly the same way as in the standard rail fence, the result is a weave pattern.

FOUR-FABRIC RAIL FENCE

If you use four different fabrics, you get a very similar effect to the standard rail fence block, but the zigzag pattern will be spaced wider apart.

STRING-PIECED RAIL FENCE

There are often odd-shaped strips of fabric left over after the rotary cutting of fabric, and string piecing is a great way to use these up. Sew the strips together along their long edges to make a pieced fabric. Press the seams to one side, then cut square blocks from the pieced fabric. Rotate the square string-pieced blocks for a random version of rail fence.

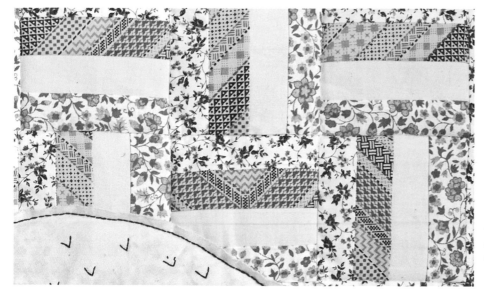

The rail fence background creates a dynamic backdrop for the owl appliqué on this lovely hanging (pages 20–25).

BRICK

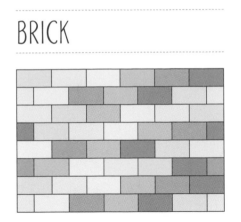

This consists of rectangles arranged in offset rows like the bricks in a wall. If you use the strip-piecing method, the bricks will be arranged symmetrically unless you unpick some seams to switch things around. If you cut and piece the rectangles individually, you can achieve a completely random effect.

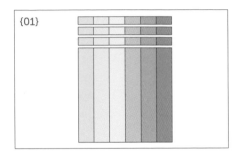

{01}

Cut many strips of different fabrics to an equal width. Stitch them together along the long edge, using a ¼" (6 mm) seam allowance. Press seams to one side, then cut the pieced strips into rows. The height of each row should be half the width of the original strips.

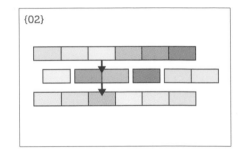

{02}

Place the rows next to one another, offsetting the seams so they fall in the center of the "brick" in the row above. To achieve a random effect, you will have to unpick some seams between "bricks" and switch them around until you get an interesting effect.

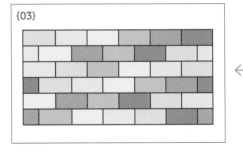

{03}

Restitch the seams. Stitch the rows together, making sure the seams stay aligned. Trim the overhangs at the edges to get a block with straight edges.

The brick pattern looks fabulous worked in bold, bright prints as seen on this curtain panel (pages 6–8).

LONDON STAIRS

If you do not unpick and rearrange some of the "bricks" before you sew the rows together, you will get a repeating steps pattern that is known as London stairs.

LOG CABIN

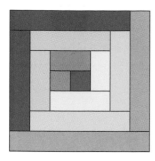

This is a very popular pattern. It is simple enough to be suitable for a beginner, but its endless possible variations mean that it is also a great favorite with more experienced patchworkers. The central square is traditionally made in a bright fabric, usually red, and represents the hearth, around which 'logs' are stitched.

SETTING PATTERNS

The basic log cabin block can be set in so many different ways to create beautiful secondary patterns. Two setting patterns are illustrated here, but there are many other possibilities.

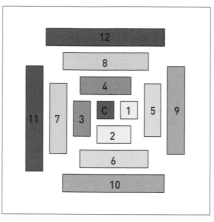

Cut strips of a selection of light and dark fabrics, all of an equal width. The central square is cut the same width as the strips. Place the central square, C, then cut another square the same size in light fabric, which will be strip 1. Strip 2 (light) and strip 3 (dark) are both twice the depth of strip 1; strip 4 (dark) and strip 5 (light) are three times the depth. Continue around in this way in

The log cabin block has been adapted to make a fantastic cushion cover using vintage bed linens (pages 47–51).

a clockwise direction, so all the light strips are on one side of the block and all the dark strips on the other. Use ¼" (6 mm) seams throughout, and press the seams in the same direction.

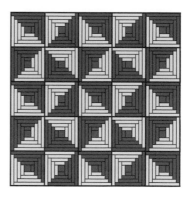

STREAK OF LIGHTNING
Zigzag lines look like streaks of lightning. If the zigzags change direction halfway across, the pattern is known as zigzags and diamonds.

PINWHEEL
If the blocks are set with light and dark sides alternating, a rotating pinwheel effect is created.

COURTHOUSE STEPS

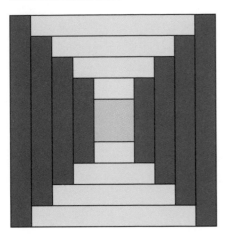

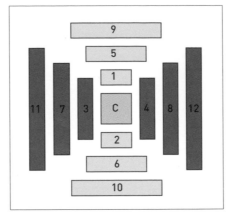

This variation on the basic log cabin block has light and dark strips arranged opposite each other. The center can have three identical squares, or a different central square flanked by two strips the same, as shown here.

Cut strips of a selection of light and dark fabrics, all of an equal width. The central square is cut the same width as the strips. Place the central square, C, then cut another two strips the same size in light fabric, which will be strips 1 and 2 (light) above and below the central square. Strips 3 and 4 (dark) are both three times the depth of the central square and go on either side. Strips 5 and 6 (light) are also three times the depth of the central square and go above and below. Continue in this way, so the lights are above and below the central square and the darks are on either side. Use ¼" (6 mm) seams throughout.

COURTHOUSE STEPS SETTING PATTERNS

The courthouse steps block is very linear, so it lends itself to being set in columns. It also combines very well with the basic log cabin block, which you might like to explore.

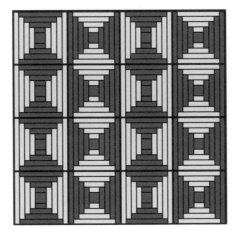

VARIATION 1
In this setting pattern the blocks are set with the light strips arranged vertically and horizontally in alternate vertical columns.

VARIATION 2
Here the blocks are alternately vertical and horizontal, which creates interesting secondary patterns.

ROMAN STRIPE

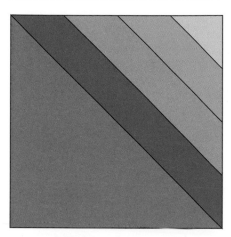

Roman stripe is a good block for the beginner to patchwork—it looks quite complex and you can make some great patterns with it, but it has no tricky points or angles to stitch.

{01}

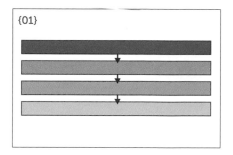

Cut strips of fabrics A, B, C and D to be used as the stripes, all of an equal width. Stitch them together along a long edge, using ¼" (6 mm) seams. Press all the seams in one direction.

{02}

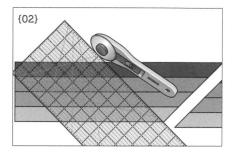

Place the pieced strip (right side up) on a cutting mat. Measure and cut one end off at a 45° angle. Swing the ruler around and cut another 45° angle, creating a right-angled triangle.

{03}

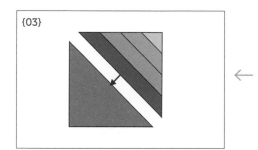

Cut a triangle the same size as the pieced triangle from a piece of plain fabric. Join the longest edge of the pieced triangle to the longest edge of the plain one but as the edge of the plain triangle will be cut on the bias, handle it with care as you are stitching the seam.

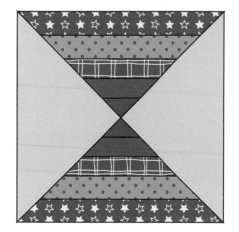

TRIANGLE BLOCK

To make this variation you need two striped triangles and two plain. This block can be set to create alternate striped and plain squares, or with alternate blocks rotated to make a pattern of triangles.

SEMINOLE

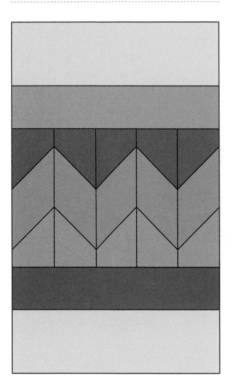

Traditional Seminole work was originally made by the women of the Seminole tribe of Native Americans based in Florida. Its key features are plain, bright colors pieced together into stripes, which are then cut and rotated to make a range of geometric patterns. More often seen on bags, the technique can be used to make beautiful and complex-looking pieced borders for quilts.

{01}

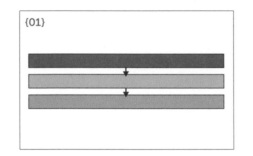

Cut strips of three brightly colored fabrics, A, B and C, all of an equal width. Stitch the strips together along the longest edges, using ¼" (6 mm) seams. Press the seams in one direction. Repeat to make a second pieced strip with the fabrics in exactly the same order.

{03}

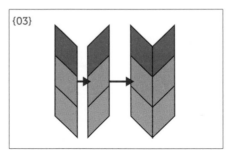

Take one length from each strip, pair them up with right sides together and with colors matching, and then stitch together along the longest edge. Repeat with all the lengths, then stitch the pieced units together to create a row with a chevron pattern.

{02}

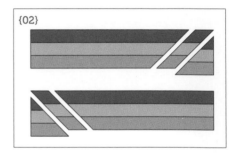

Cut the end of the first pieced strip at a 45° angle at the right-hand end, then cut at the same angle at intervals along the length to create several equal lengths. Cut the second strip at a 45° angle at the opposite end, then cut at the same angle at intervals along the length to create several equal lengths.

Note

Since the pieces of fabric used are quite small and are cut apart at an angle, Seminole work is usually made in plain, bright colors, although very small print designs are sometimes used, as on the Seminole diamond camera case (pages 66–71).

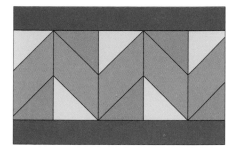

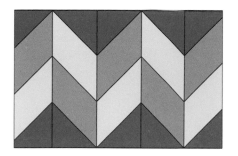

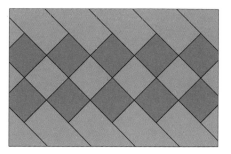

SINGLE CHEVRON

Although it looks quite different, this design has been created in exactly the same way as in the steps opposite, but the two lengths are rotated alternately, so the darker color is first at the bottom and then at the top. This makes the central zigzag much more prominent.

DOUBLE CHEVRON

This block uses four fabrics, with the same one used both top and bottom. When the lengths are rotated alternately, the central diagonal lines create a checkerboard design.

DIAMONDS

To make this design, cut two wide strips in the main fabric, then three narrow strips, one in the main fabric and two in the contrast fabric. Piece the strips together so the two wide strips are at the ends and the three narrow ones alternate in the middle. Square off one end of the pieced strip, then slice off lengths that are each the same width as one of the inner stripes. Piece these lengths together, staggering the central squares, then turn so the squares are on point and trim across all the edges to square up the block.

The front and back panels of the camera case are made from bands of Seminole diamond pattern using four different colored fabric strips.

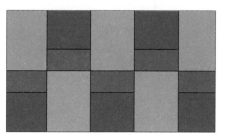

STEPS

Piecing three strips of fabric of different widths makes this simple but effective pattern. Slice the pieced strip into lengths, then alternate the lengths to create the stepped pattern and stitch together again.

NINE-PATCH

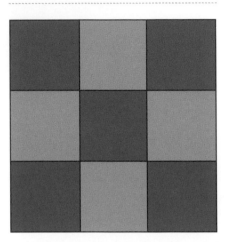

The popular nine-patch can either be strip-pieced, as shown here, or made from individual squares as shown for four-patch on page 114. The way the colors are placed can change the look entirely, and it is an ideal block for using up odd scraps of fabric.

Four different fabrics were used for the nine-patch panels on the top and base of the beanbag on pages 6–9.

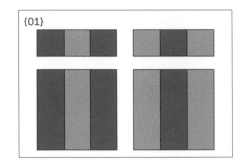

{01}

Cut three strips each of fabrics A and B, making each strip one-third of the finished block width plus ⅜" (1 cm) for seam allowances. Take two strips of A and one of B and piece together alternately. Piece together the remaining three strips. You should now have two pieced strips, one ABA and the other BAB. Stitch the sets of three strips together along the long edge, using a ¼" (6 mm) seam. Press seams to one side. Cut both of the finished pieced strips into rows, with each row one-third of the finished block width plus ⅜" (1 cm) for seam allowances.

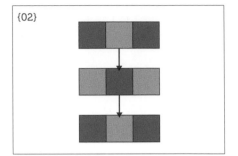

{02}

Take two rows from the first pieced strip and one from the second, and lay them in alternate order. Stitch the rows together with a ¼" (6 mm) seam.

DOUBLE NINE-PATCH

This nine-patch within a nine-patch is made of five small nine-patch blocks joined together in a large nine-patch block, with plain squares in between. When several of these blocks are set together, the small squares create a diagonal grid across the quilt.

IRISH CHAIN

The Irish chain pattern makes a great beginner's design. It has many variations including double Irish chain, which is illustrated here. It is constructed from two different blocks, and when the blocks are joined together, a diagonal grid of chains begins to develop across the quilt.

Note

When making an Irish chain quilt, remember that you are using two different blocks to make up the pattern, so you will need to plan the quilt using an odd number of blocks both across and down to make sure the design is centered on the quilt. The four corner blocks must be the same pattern, and there should be one block at the center.

DOUBLE IRISH CHAIN

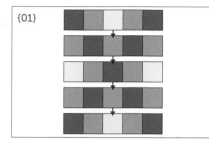

Making the first block:
Cut strips of fabrics A, B and C, each one-fifth the width of the finished block plus ⅜" (1 cm) for seam allowances. Join the strips together with ¼" (6 mm) seams, working in three different orders: ABCBA, BABAB and CBABC. Cut each pieced strip into rows one-fifth the width of the finished block plus ⅜" (1 cm) for seam allowances. Stitch five rows together in the order shown, with ¼" (6 mm) seams.

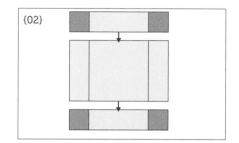

Making the second block:
Cut a center square from fabric C that is three-fifths the width of the finished block plus ⅜" (1 cm) for seam allowances. Cut four strips from fabric C, each one-fifth the width of the finished block plus ⅜" (1 cm) for seam allowances, and a length equal to three-fifths the width of the finished block plus ⅜" (1 cm) for seam allowances. Cut four squares from fabric B, one-fifth the width of the finished block plus ⅜" (1 cm) for seam allowances. Join these pieces into rows as shown, using a ¼" (6 mm) seam, and then into a block.

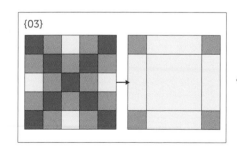

Join the pairs of blocks together using a ¼" (6 mm) seam, matching seams carefully across the join.

Piecing with squares and triangles

{ Squares are the basis for some of the oldest patchwork patterns and are as simple to work as strips, since you are only working with straight seams. If you cut a square in half diagonally you get a right-angled triangle, and many traditional patterns are based on these two shapes, either used alone or combined.

FOUR-PATCH

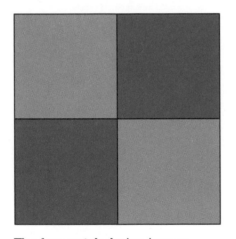

The four-patch design is very straightforward and easy to make, but it can be made to look very different depending on the placement of the fabrics and the way the blocks are pieced together. The squares can be combined as shown here, or using the strip-piecing method illustrated for the nine-patch block on page 112.

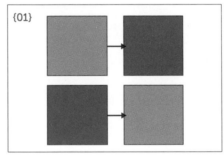

{01}

Cut two equal-sized squares in each of fabrics A and B. Use a ¼" (6 mm) seam and join each A square to a B square.

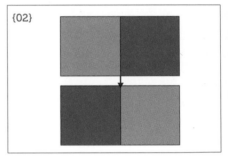

{02}

Matching the center seam carefully, join the two pairs together, with A next to B.

Note

Four-patch may look quite simple, but a large number of much more intricate designs are based upon it. The individual squares can be made up using combinations of other shapes, as in broken dishes and its variations (page 118) and drunkard's path patterns (pages 134–135).

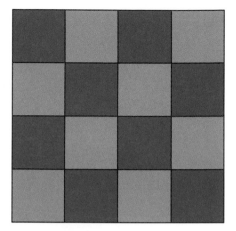

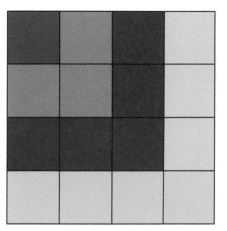

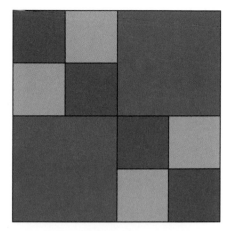

DOUBLE FOUR-PATCH

Also known as sixteen-patch, this block is created by joining four four-patch blocks. If you use two contrasting colors the effect created will be a checkerboard, as here, but if the colors tone the result will be more like a mosaic pattern (page 124).

Note

If you are a beginner, the four-patch block is a great way to practice achieving a ¼" (6 mm) seam and to achieving perfect alignment where seams meet.

DOUBLE FOUR-PATCH VARIATION

This block uses four different fabrics, but contains only two different four-patch designs. The top left and bottom right are the same layout—each has a square in one fabric combined with three others in a different fabric. The other two four-patch blocks are identical—just rotated. The block can be set in several ways: in lines, creating a series of chevrons; in rotation to make concentric squares; or on point to look like an abstract flower. If you add plain squares, the possibilities multiply further.

FOUR-PATCH AND SQUARES

This simple, but effective block is made from two four-patch squares joined with two plain squares. The use of plain squares in the design creates a perfect space for quilting motifs.

The individual squares of a four-patch can be made up using combinations of other shapes, as in broken dishes and its variations as seen on the floor cushion design (pages 34–39)

FRIENDSHIP STAR

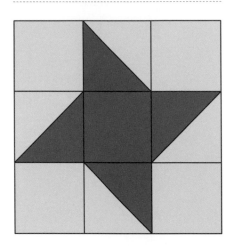

Although at first glance this block looks quite complex, in fact it is a simple variation on the standard nine-patch. It is made of squares and right-angled triangles, so it is easy to cut the shapes. Depending on how the fabrics are placed within the design, the result can look quite different.

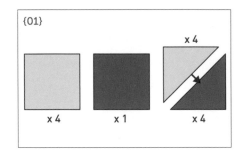

Cut two squares of fabric A and two of B, and cut them in half diagonally to get four right-angled triangles in each fabric. Take one A triangle and one B triangle and join them along the diagonal, using a ¼" (6 mm) seam. Repeat with the other triangles to make four triangle squares. Use one completed unit as a template to cut four plain squares the same size from fabric A and one from fabric B.

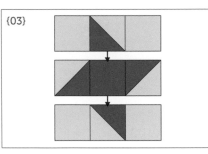

Match the seams across the rows and then stitch the three rows together, again using a ¼" (6 mm) seam.

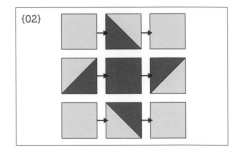

Arrange the squares as shown in the diagram. Stitch the top row of three together, using a ¼" (6 mm) seam, then stitch the middle and bottom rows in the same way. Press seams to one side.

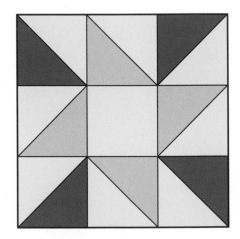

NINE-PATCH STAR

This block is made in the same way as shown in the steps above, but the four corner squares are pieced using a contrasting third fabric, which gives a lively rotating effect.

PINWHEEL

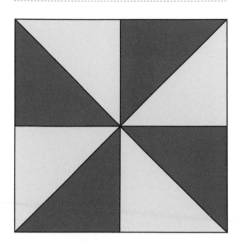

The triangles in this four-patch block are set so they rotate around the center, creating a block called pinwheel, windmill or flutter blades. The design is always full of movement and vitality and can be set in several different ways. There are also many possible variations on the basic block.

Note

The orientation of the triangles is critical when making pinwheel blocks. Lay out the pieces before beginning to stitch, and check the block as you work to make sure that the "blades" are all rotating in the correct direction.

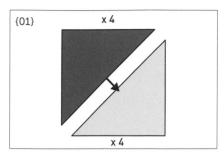

Cut two squares from fabric A and two from fabric B. Cut each in half along the diagonal to make four right-angled triangles in each fabric. Take one triangle of A and one of B and join along the diagonal, using a ¼" (6 mm) seam. Press the seam to one side. Repeat with the other triangles.

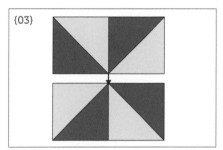

Match the seams carefully in the center, and pin before stitching the two rows together.

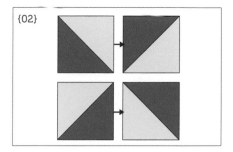

Arrange the triangle squares so that the triangles rotate. Stitch the top two squares together, then stitch the bottom two together.

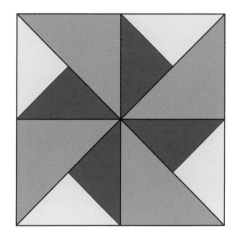

DOUBLE PINWHEEL

The double pinwheel uses three fabrics and creates a spiral within a spiral. Each alternate blade is pieced from two triangles. There is a variation on this block called turnstile: in this the large blades and the outer small triangles are in the same color.

BROKEN DISHES

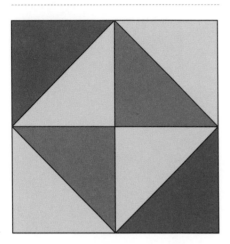

This block is based on a simple four-patch. Traditionally, four of the units shown here are joined together to make one big block and then this block is set alternately with a plain one the same size. If several tones of the same two colors are used, a gloriously fragmented effect can be achieved.

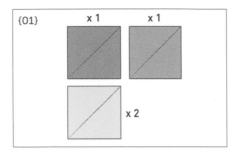

For each block cut one square each of fabrics A and B, and two squares of fabric C. Mark a diagonal line on the wrong side of all the blocks, being careful not to stretch the fabric out of shape on the bias.

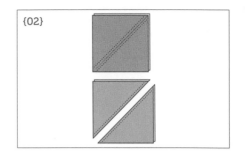

With right sides together, place an A square on top of a C square and a B square on top of the other C square, matching the diagonal lines. Stitch ¼" (6 mm) away from the line down one side, then turn and come back ¼" (6 mm) away down the other side. Cut along the diagonal line between the stitching lines.

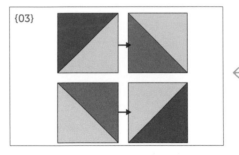

Press the triangle squares flat with the seams to one side. Take two of the triangle squares, one with fabric A and one with fabric B, and join them together as shown. Repeat with the other two triangle squares. Matching seams, join the two pairs together into a block.

SOUTHERN BELLE

This lively design has a center made in exactly the same way as a basic broken dishes block. However, the outer triangles are further divided into smaller right-angled triangles, which gives the block a sense of rotating movement.

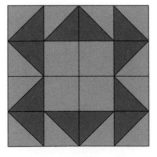

BUZZARD'S ROOST

The center of this block is made of four plain squares, but apart from this it uses triangle squares. When set in rows, the dark triangles at the sides will combine to make squares set on point.

SHOOFLY

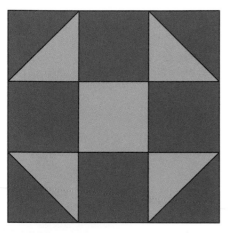

The shoofly block is a nine-patch variation made from squares and triangle squares, so it is a very easy block to piece. The plain squares are broken down further in some variations and it is also very effective set on point (see Setting Patterns, page 140).

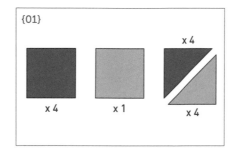

{01}

Cut two squares from fabric A and two from fabric B. Cut each in half along the diagonal to make four right-angled triangles in each fabric. Take one triangle of A and one of B and join along the diagonal, using a ¼" (6 mm) seam. Press the seam to one side. Repeat with the other triangles. Using one completed triangle square as a template, cut four squares the same size from fabric A and one from fabric B.

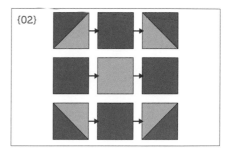

{02}

Place the nine squares in three rows, with the triangle squares in the corners and the square of fabric B in the center. Join the squares into three rows using ¼" (6 mm) seams. Press all the seams to one side.

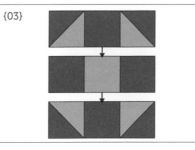

{03}

Matching the seams carefully, join the three rows into a block.

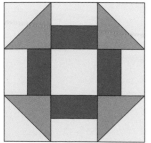

CHURN DASH

This simple variation of shoofly has the central squares on each side pieced from two equal-width strips of different fabrics.

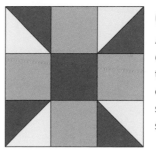

CALICO PUZZLE

Although this design looks quite different, it is constructed in exactly the same way as the shoofly block, except that the corner triangle squares are rotated so the diagonal seam runs toward the center.

SNAIL'S TRAIL

One of the interesting features of this block is the visual effect of curving lines that is created purely by using larger and larger triangles spiraling out around the center. It is most effective made in two highly contrasting fabrics, although some interesting variations occur when other colors are added. A series of snail's trail blocks in just three colors set in a row would give a wonderful impression of breaking waves.

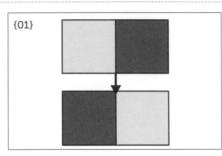

{01}

Cut two small squares from fabric A and two from fabric B. Stitch two different squares together, then stitch the units to one another to create a small four-patch block.

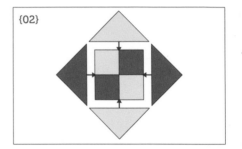

{02}

Cut a square of fabric A and of fabric B so the diagonal of each square is the length of the side of the four-patch block, plus ¼" (6 mm) seam allowance. Cut the squares diagonally to make two right-angled triangles from each square. Add a triangle of fabric A at the top and bottom of the four-patch block. Add triangles of fabric B on each side.

MONKEY WRENCH

This design uses four different colors, but is created in exactly the same way as snail's trail. When blocks like this are set together, unusual secondary patterns can be created across the quilt.

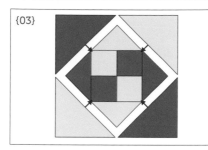

Cut another square of fabric A and of fabric B so the diagonal of each square is the length of the side of the block made so far, plus ¼" (6 mm) seam allowance. Cut the squares diagonally to make two right-angled triangles from each square. Add the next row of triangles, keeping both A and B triangles opposite each other. Carry on in this way, making the triangles bigger each time to match the sides of the block—the final block has four different sized triangles, with two of each size in each color.

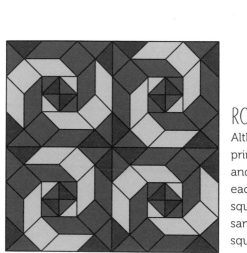

The spiral-effect achieved when blocks of snail's trail are placed together can be clearly seen on this detail from the snail's trail quilt (pages 61–65).

ROUGH SEA

Although this pattern is constructed using the same principle as snail's trail, it uses a wider variety of shapes and is more difficult to piece. The central square in each block is pieced from four triangles instead of four squares, and the next row of surrounding triangles is the same size. After that come alternate parallelograms and squares, finishing with triangles in each corner.

SAWTOOTH

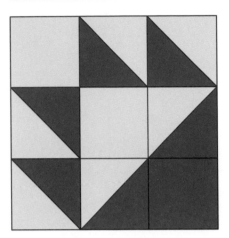

The jagged teeth of the sawtooth block add a look of great complexity to any quilt design, but it is simply made from triangles and squares. In the example shown here, it is constructed as a nine-patch block, but the teeth can also be used to edge other shapes.

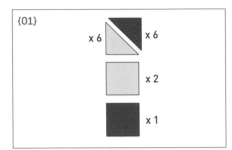

{01}

x 6   x 6

x 2

x 1

Cut three squares from fabric A and three from fabric B. Cut each in half along the diagonal to make six right-angled triangles in each fabric. Take one triangle of A and one of B and join along the diagonal, using a ¼" (6 mm) seam. Press the seam to one side. Repeat with the other triangles. Using a finished triangle square as a template, cut two squares the same size from fabric A and one from fabric B.

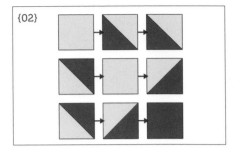

{02}

Arrange the nine squares in three rows of three. Stitch each row of three squares together into a strip, using ¼" (6 mm) seams. Press the seams in opposite directions on each row.

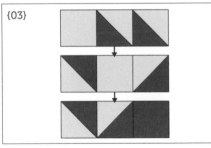

{03}

Matching the seam lines and points carefully, join the three rows together into a block.

SAWTOOTH ROWS

This design couldn't be simpler—it's just four identical rows of triangle squares. It would be an ideal design for using up your fabric scraps.

 PATCHWORK

FLYING GEESE

The flying geese unit is always twice as wide as it is high. The finished units can be joined to create bars, which make excellent borders for quilts, or when alternated with strips of plain fabric a lovely strippy quilt can be made.

Note

A flying geese unit is made up of a larger triangle, which represents the goose, and two smaller triangles, which represent the sky. To make your geese stand out, choose fabrics with a good light/dark contrast for these two elements.

The pinwheel blocks that form the center band of the tote bag (pages 40–46) are made from four flying geese units.

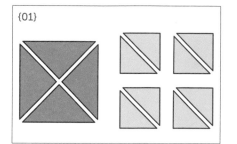

{01}

Cut one square in fabric A the size of the finished width of the block plus 1¼" (3 cm). Cut this diagonally into four triangles. Cut four squares in fabric B the height of the finished block (i.e. half the width) plus ⅞" (2.2 cm). Cut each small square diagonally into two triangles.

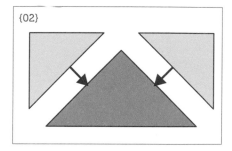

{02}

Using ¼" (6 mm) seams, sew a triangle in fabric B to the top two angled sides of the triangle in fabric A. Press the seams to one side. Repeat until all four units are made.

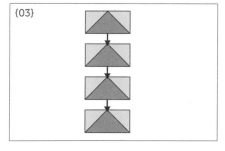

{03}

Stitch each flying geese block to the next one, using ¼" (6 mm) seams. Press the seams to one side. Repeat steps until you have the length of bar you need.

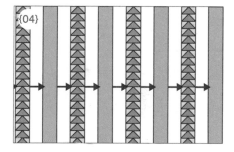

{04}

To make a quilt, bars of flying geese can be joined alternately to plain fabric bars (shown as blue strips in the diagram above). To finish, add a border on all four sides, complete with batting, backing and binding (see Making a Patchwork Quilt, pages 139–152). This type of quilt is referred to as a strippy quilt. You can get creative with your quilting patterns on the plain strips, or just quilt in-the-ditch down the edge of each strip.

Mosaic pattern piecing

This selection of patterns gets its name from the fact that, just as small pieces of stone, ceramic or glass can be combined to create decorative patterns, so too can small pieces of fabric. It is amazing what you can do with small squares, hexagons and diamonds, and they are a great way to use up fabric scraps.

POSTAGE STAMP

Traditionally, the postage stamp design is created from scraps, with the colors and patterns placed randomly. The technique shown here is for strip-piecing a random design. However, the tiny squares can also be arranged to create repeating patterns, as shown in the variations.

{01}

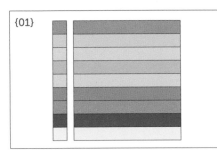

Cut narrow strips of nine different fabrics, all of an equal width. Stitch the strips together along their width, with a ¼" (6 mm) seam allowance. Press all the seams to one side. Cut a length from one end of the pieced strips to get a row of equal sized squares. Repeat until you have nine rows of squares.

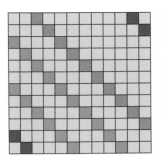

{02}

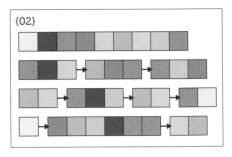

Lay the rows of squares next to one another. Cut some of the rows apart and rotate some sections to achieve a random effect. Stitch the cut rows back together again, then stitch the rows together, matching seams carefully, to create a block.

KITE TAILS

This design can either be created using the strip-piecing method shown for the basic postage stamp block, or by joining the squares into rows and then the rows into blocks.

GRANDMOTHER'S FLOWER GARDEN

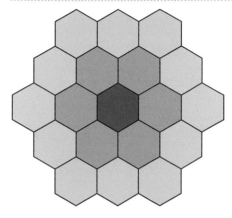

The hexagon is one of the basic geometric shapes, and hexagons can easily be joined together to create wonderful patterns. The simplest way of working this shape is to use the English paper-piecing method (see page 94).

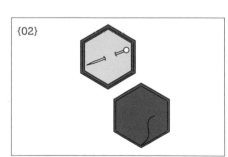

{02}

Pin a paper hexagon to the wrong side of each fabric hexagon. Fold the seam allowance marked on the fabric over the edge of the paper shape all around and press, then baste the fabric in position.

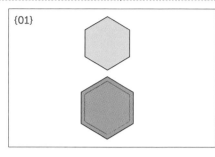

{01}

Use the hexagon template on page 156. Cut 19 hexagons from paper, using the inner line of the hexagon. Using the outer line of the template, cut one hexagon in fabric A, six in fabric B and 12 in fabric C. Mark a ¼" (6 mm) seam allowance on the wrong side of all the fabric pieces.

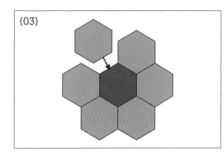

{03}

With the hexagon in fabric A at the center, add a hexagon in fabric B to each side, whipstitching the seam. When all the hexagons are in place, whipstitch the seam between adjoining B hexagons. Repeat this with the outer row of C hexagons.

To make a block with a diamond shape, simply add another fabric B hexagon to the top and bottom of the shape in step 3.

TUMBLING BLOCKS

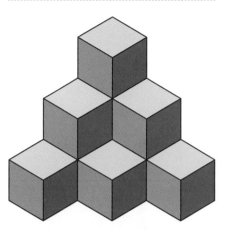

This pattern has a dramatic 3D effect when made in dark, medium and light fabrics.

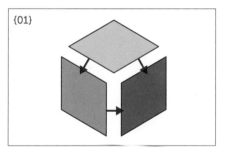

{01}

Cut three diamonds (see Templates, page 153) from paper for each unit, using the inner line. Using the outer line, cut one diamond in fabric A, one in fabric B and one in fabric C. Mark a ¼" (6 mm) seam allowance on the wrong side of the fabric pieces and pin a paper diamond to the wrong side of each. Fold the seam allowance over the edge of the paper shape all around. Press, then baste in position. Whipstitch the diamonds together to make one unit.

Star pattern piecing

Star patterns come in many different types and sizes. The simplest designs have only four or six points, while some can have 32 or even more. Since all the seams are straight, many star patterns can be pieced by machine—although joining the points at the center is always fiddly.

BLAZING STAR

This is a type of four-pointed star. The simplest way to keep the points neat and the bias seams straight is to use the English paper-piecing method (page 94) for its construction.

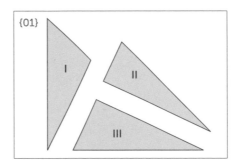

{01}

Using the template on page 153, cut eight triangles from paper in each of shapes I, II and III. Using the outer line of template I, cut four triangles in fabric A and four in fabric B. Using the outer line of template II, cut four triangles in fabric C and four in fabric D. Using the outer line of template III, cut eight triangles in fabric E. Mark a ¼" (6 mm) seam allowance on the wrong side of all the fabric pieces. Pin a matching paper triangle to the wrong side of each fabric piece.

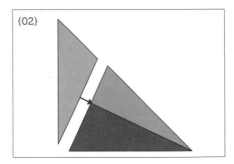

{02}

Fold the seam allowance marked on the fabric over the edge of the paper shape all around and press, then baste in position. Join four triangles in fabric E to triangles in fabric C. Join the remaining four triangles in E to the triangles in fabric D. Add a triangle in fabric A to the end of each E/C unit and a triangle in fabric B to the end of each D/E unit. Check the picture of the block regularly to make sure you are adding the colors in the right place.

The giant rainbow star quilt (pages 14–19) takes its inspiration from traditional star pattern patchwork blocks.

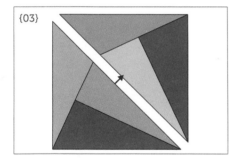

{03}

Take two different units and join them together to make a square block. Repeat with the other units so you have four identical square blocks. Finally, join the squares as for a four-patch block (see page 114), being very careful to keep the points sharp at the center.

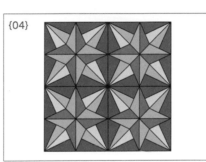

{04}

This diagram shows the effect of several blazing star blocks combined directly. As often happens, a secondary pattern emerges—here an almost circular shape can be seen in the center of the pattern. The use of different colors can make this effect more prominent.

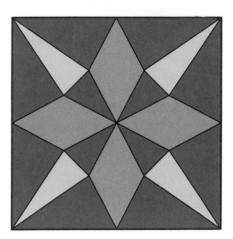

NORTH STAR

This variation of blazing star uses triangles and diamonds, but is made in basically the same way. The small center triangles could be made in the same fabric as the long points, giving a cross effect, or in the same fabric as the large points, making the central star more prominent.

EIGHT-POINTED STAR

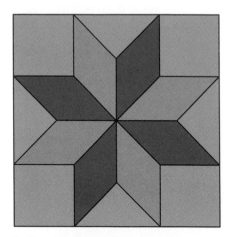

In its simplest form, the eight-pointed star is made from diamonds in two alternating colors, with triangles and squares to fill in around the edges. With eight seams meeting in the middle, it can be tricky to keep the points sharp and the seams aligned.

Use the diamond and right-angled triangle templates on page 153, and make up a square template to fit in the angle of two diamonds as shown in step 2. Draw an inner line ¼" (5 mm) in from the edge all around the square template. Cut eight diamonds, four triangles and four squares from paper, using the inner line. Using the outer line of the template, cut four squares in fabric A, four triangles in fabric A, four diamonds in fabric B and four in fabric C. Mark a ¼" (5 mm) seam allowance on the wrong side of

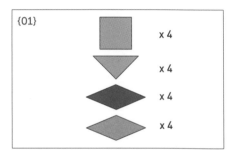

{01}

x 4

x 4

x 4

x 4

all the fabric pieces. Pin a matching paper shape to the wrong side of each fabric piece. Fold the seam allowance marked on the fabric over the edge of the paper shape all around and press, then baste in position.

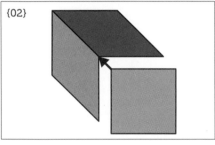

{02}

Using a ¼" (5 mm) seam, stitch two diamonds together along one edge. Repeat to make four pairs of diamonds. Add a square in the angle made by each paired diamond unit, sewing from the center point outward each time. Stitch two completed pairs together, then stitch the two units together into the star.

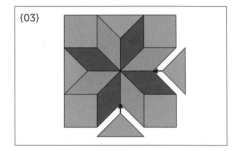

{03}

Add the triangles on the sides, using a ¼" (5 mm) seam and stitching from the inner point outward each time. Press the seams open.

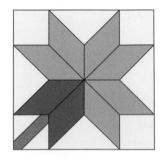

To make the star into a stylized flower adjust the colors used and add an appliqué stem.

OHIO STAR

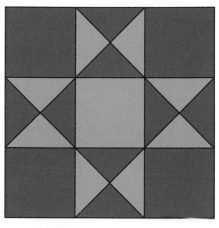

The Ohio star block is a popular pattern that is quick to piece and has many variations. It is constructed using only two shapes—a square and a quarter-triangle. The finished block looks quite intricate on its own, so it is generally set simply with plain spacer blocks, or just in rows with plain sashing.

Note

If your quarter-triangles do not come out as a perfect crossed square—despite accurate cutting and stitching—try cutting them a little bit bigger, then stitch and trim to size.

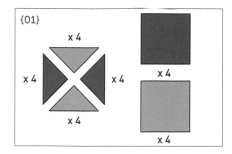

{01}

Cut two squares in each of fabrics A and B. Cut each square across on both diagonals to make four right-angled triangles, eight in each fabric. Take two triangles in each color and piece into a new square as shown. Repeat with the other triangles. Press the finished squares and use one as a template to cut four squares the same size in fabric A and one in fabric B.

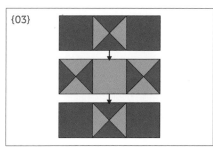

{03}

Join the rows together, matching both vertical and diagonal seams carefully. Press seams to one side.

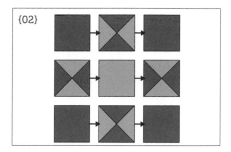

{02}

Arrange the squares in rows, with the top and bottom line running A–pieced square–A and the middle row running pieced square–B–pieced square. Join the squares together, using ¼" (5 mm) seams. Press seams to one side.

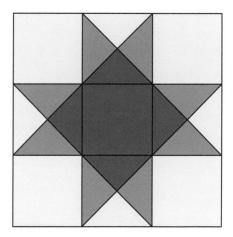

VARIABLE STAR

This block is constructed in the same way as the basic Ohio star block using three fabrics, so that the square in the center and its surrounding triangles read as a square set on point.

Piecing with curves

Designs based on curves are often intricate and may be difficult to stitch by machine, unless the curves are very gentle. Despite this, they are popular because beautiful designs with swirling shapes, full of vitality, can be created. Many patterns are also ideal for using up odd shaped scraps of fabric.

CLAMSHELL

This is a very traditional pattern, but it is rather complicated to construct. The easiest method is to use English paper piecing (page 94) as described here.

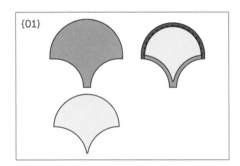

{01}

Use the clamshell template on page 154 to cut several clamshells from paper. Make a second template, adding an extra ¼" (6 mm) seam allowance all around, and use this to cut a selection of clamshells in various fabrics. Mark a ¼" (6 mm) seam allowance on the wrong side of all fabric pieces. Pin a paper shape to the wrong side of each fabric piece. Fold the fabric's seam allowance over the edges of the paper. Press, then baste in position. Mark the center top on each clamshell.

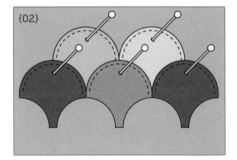

{02}

Use a spare paper clamshell template to draw a row of curves across the bottom of a piece of thick card or a pinboard. Pin a row of fabric patches in position along the scalloped line. Add a second row staggered above the first, adjusting the position of colors until you are totally happy with the design.

The clamshell fabric pieces of the
iPad sleeve (pages 52–55) were
fussy cut from retro-inspired fabrics.

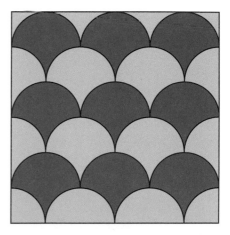

CLAMSHELL VARIATION

For a different effect, try working the
rows in just two alternating colors.

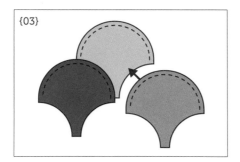

{03}

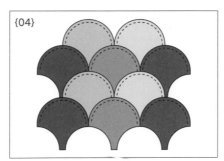

{04}

Make sure the edge of the first patch
in the second row aligns with the
marked center top point on the first
patch in the bottom row. Slip stitch the
two patches together, starting at the
center top point and stitching along
the seam line of the lower curve of the
bottom patch. Add the next patch in
the bottom row in the same way.

Keep repeating this sequence, adding
alternate patches from the top and
bottom rows. When you have stitched
all the patches on the pinboard, pin
another two rows in place and then
start again.

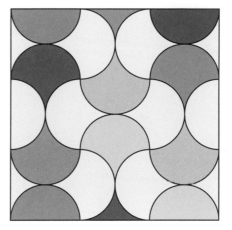

SHELL PATCHWORK

The double curves of the clamshell
shape fit into one another, so if
the patches are rotated so that the
points face one another, two further
clamshells can be used to fill in the
gaps on each side. This creates an
interesting curvy mosaic.

FAN

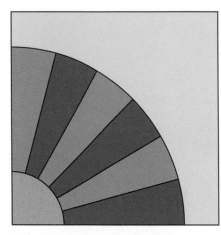

This fan design has many variations. The fan itself can have many more blades, and four fan blocks together create the well-known design called Dresden plate. Rotating the fan blocks can create interesting secondary patterns across a quilt design.

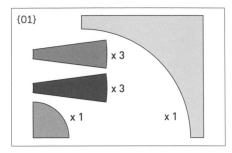

{01}

Use the fan templates on page 153. Using template I, cut three blades in fabric A and three blades in fabric B. Using template II, cut one corner piece in fabric C. Using template III, cut one background piece in fabric D.

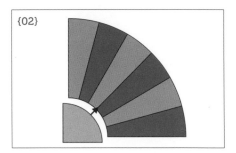

{02}

Using a ¼" (6 mm) seam, stitch one blade A to one blade B. Repeat with the other two pairs, then stitch the pairs together into the fan. Press the seams open, or to one side. Add the corner piece, being very careful not to stretch the curved seam as you stitch.

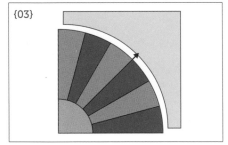

{03}

Add the background piece, again being very careful not to stretch the curved seam as you stitch. You can stitch this by hand or machine, but it must lie perfectly flat. Clip the curved seam if necessary.

Note

The corner piece can also be made as an appliqué to cover the pointed ends of the blades running right down into the corner. The blades should alternate in color to get the best result from the fan design, but you can use many more than two colors if you wish, which is a great way to use up scraps.

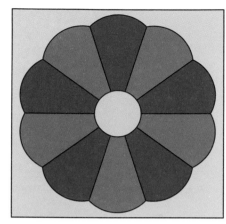

SIMPLE DRESDEN PLATE

The large segments and limited number of colors make this very simple Dresden plate quite easy to stitch. If you make the central circle as an appliqué you don't have to worry about the central points meeting perfectly.

DRESDEN PLATE

This more traditional version of Dresden plate uses three fabrics for the plate design, and two shapes—rounded and pointed.

The Dresden plate appliquéd on to the front panel of the tea cozy (pages 26–29) has pointed blades only, cut from many different fabric scraps.

DRUNKARD'S PATH

Drunkard's path patterns use a square with a quarter-circle in a contrasting color across one corner. This square can be set in many ways to create an endless series of variations. The staggered look of the design is supposed to recall a drunkard staggering home.

Note

When machine stitching curved (bias) seams, work with great care so that you do not stretch the fabric as you pull it through the sewing machine. It is often a good idea to cut notches on matching curved edges, so you have fixed points to work with.

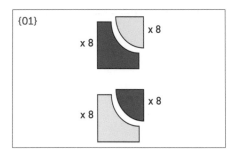

{01}
x 8
x 8
x 8
x 8

Using the templates on page 155, cut eight pieces of each shape in fabric A and eight in fabric B. Join the small pieces in fabric A to the large pieces in fabric B and vice versa, so you have 16 squares, each with a contrast section across one corner. Clip curves in the seam allowances and press all the seams flat.

{02}

Lay out the 16 squares as shown. Join the pairs together first to make eight pairs of squares, following the diagram above closely. Join the pairs together to create four pieced blocks.

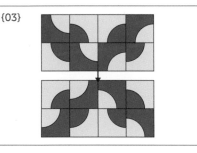

{03}

Join the four squares together, matching seams across joins carefully, following the instructions for a four-patch block on page 114.

{04}

When you combine several drunkard's path blocks without sashing, complex patterns and sinuous curves begin to develop.

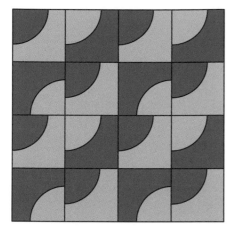

FALLING TIMBERS

This design uses exactly the same elements and techniques as the basic drunkard's path block, but the squares are orientated to run in diagonal lines. Worked in greens and browns, the diagonal lines look like fallen trees in the forest.

WONDER OF THE WORLD

To make this variation, use four dark squares with light corners, and 12 light ones with dark corners.

Quarter-circle units, the key components of the drunkard's path patchwork pattern, have been combined with simple squares to create the floral motif on the placemats (page 80).

Appliqué techniques

Appliqué is the decorative technique of applying cut-out fabric pieces or motifs to a background fabric. It can be a great way to add detail to a patchwork background as seen on the nine-patch bean bag. The fabric used and the effect you are aiming for will dictate which appliqué technique to use.

CUT-AND-SEW HAND APPLIQUÉ

Also known as folk art appliqué or raw-edge appliqué, this is the most basic form of appliqué. It works well with felt or when you are using a fabric backed with iron-on interfacing to stop it fraying. It is particularly good for small or irregular shapes.

Draw the motif directly on the fabric, or make a template of the shape and draw around it. Cut out all the shapes with sharp scissors.

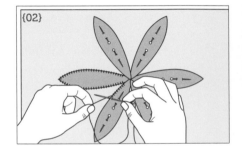

Use a suitable embroidery stitch to stitch the motif to the background fabric: backstitch, whipstitch and blanket stitch are all good options.

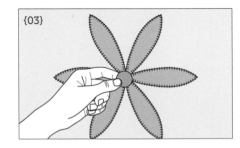

Here, where the petals meet in the center there is a ragged gap at their ends, so a small circle of fabric, in a different color, was added to represent the flower center.

The motif can easily be further embellished by adding more embroidery, but it looks just as good if it is left fairly plain.

TURNED-EDGE HAND APPLIQUÉ

In turned-edge hand appliqué (sometimes called needle-turn appliqué), the edge of the motif is turned under with the very tip of the needle as you work. Mark your appliqué motif onto the right side of the fabric and cut out leaving a border ¼" (6 mm) all the way around the outside of the marked line. You can also use freezer paper to press under a seam allowance.

Note

If you cannot to find a thread that exactly matches the fabric used for the motif, the rule of thumb is to choose one a shade lighter if you are appliquéing to a light background, but select a shade darker if you are appliquéing to a dark background. Keep the stitches as small and neat as possible—they should barely show, unless of course you are working folk art appliqué with a decorative embroidery stitch.

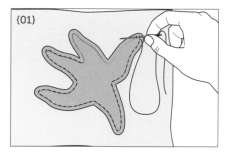

{01}

Place the motif, right side up, on the right side of the background fabric. Baste it in position, stitching about ¼" (6 mm) inside the marked line.

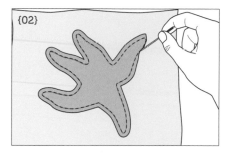

{02}

Use the point of the needle to turn under a short section of the motif's edge, until the raw edge meets the basting line. Slip stitch the folded edge to the background fabric, then turn under the next section. Continue in this way until the motif is stitched all the way round. (If the edge of an appliqué piece will be covered by another piece that is going to be added later, there is no need to turn the edge under.)

{03}

Remove the basting stitches and gently press the motif from the wrong side. On the right side, the edges of the motif will be smooth.

FREEZER PAPER HAND APPLIQUÉ

Freezer paper is useful for the turned-edge hand appliqué technique, helping you to turn under the seam allowance accurately and neatly.

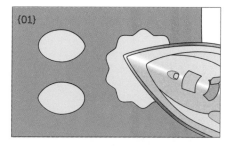

{01}

Make a template for each shape. Place each template on the paper side of the freezer paper, draw around it and then cut out the shapes. Place the appliqué fabric, wrong side up, with the freezer paper shapes (sticky side down) on top. Iron the paper in place. Cut out the shapes, leaving a ¼" (6 mm) seam allowance all around.

{02}

Snip into any concave edges or inner corners. Press the seam allowance to the wrong side, over the edge of the freezer paper. Peel off the freezer paper. Now slip stitch the appliqué to the background using matching thread and small stitches.

FUSED APPLIQUÉ

Fusible web has made appliqué much quicker and easier, and it is particularly good for working with complicated shapes. You need to remember that because you are working on the back of the fabric, the motif will be reversed when it is right side up, so take this into account if your appliqué motif is non-symmetrical or features letters or numbers.

Note

To appliqué with your sewing machine, you will need a machine with a good zigzag stitch that can be worked closely, like satin stitch. Many machines also have other decorative stitches that can be used for appliqué.

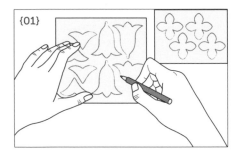

{01}

Trace all the appliqué shapes on to the paper backing of the fusible web—the shapes can be quite close together to save on materials. You should aim to group pieces in the same color and cut them out in one block.

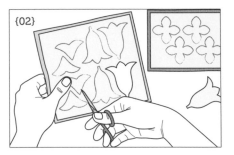

{02}

Iron your blocks of motifs to the reverse side of your appliqué fabrics. Carefully cut out around each of the appliqué motifs.

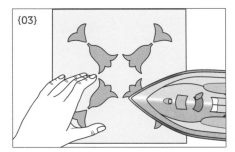

{03}

Peel off the backing paper and carefully place the first pieces on the background fabric. Iron into position.

{04}

Add the remaining pieces and iron into place. To secure the pieces in place you can hand embroider or machine stitch around the edges if you wish.

Making a patchwork quilt

Patchwork blocks are most often used to create a decorative top to make a bed quilt. A quilt is generally made from two layers of fabric with padding in between, with the layers held together with quilting stitches or ties. Why not turn your practice blocks into a beautiful accessory for the home?

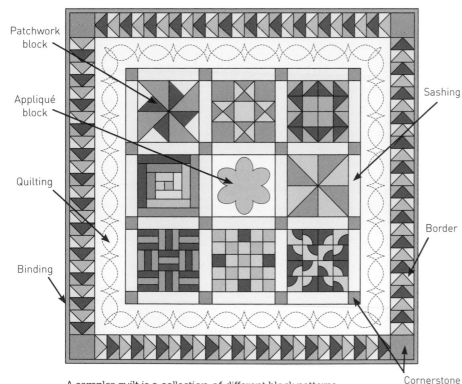

Patchwork block

Appliqué block

Quilting

Binding

Sashing

Border

Cornerstone

A sampler quilt is a collection of different block patterns made up into one quilt. It's considered a good starter quilt for beginners, as they can begin with the easiest block and progress to the more difficult.

Patchwork quilt glossary

Block: A unit composed of patchwork or appliqué pieces. Usually square, blocks can be combined to make a quilt.

Quilting: A type of running stitch that holds quilt layers together permanently.

Border: A strip of fabric sewn to the outer edges of a quilt top to serve as a frame for the interior, or to enhance the design.

Cornerstone: The fabric squares often used where border/sashing strips meet.

Sashing: Strips of fabric sewn between pieced blocks to separate them when joining them together into a quilt top.

Binding: A strip of fabric sewn over the edges of a quilt to finish the raw edges and/or decorate the edge.

Quilt sandwich: A term quilters use to describe a quilt top, batting and backing layered together.

JOINING BLOCKS

A block can either be a plain spacer unit, a pieced patchwork block, or an appliqué block, and the way blocks are arranged in a quilt top is called the setting pattern. Quilt blocks that are incorporated with their corners pointing up and down in a diamond shape are described as set "on point."

FIG A

SETTING PATTERNS

"Setting" describes the way you put separate blocks together to create a complete quilt. A block can either be a plain spacer unit, a pieced patchwork block, or an appliqué block. You may have many blocks in an identical design, or a mixture of blocks that must be placed together in a logical way. If the blocks are set block to block—or joined directly to each other—many different secondary patterns can often be created (see fig A below).

Alternatively, individual blocks can be set with lines of sashing between them (fig B), which is a way to eke out a limited number of blocks into a larger quilt. When quilt blocks are put into a quilt with their corners pointing up and down—in a diamond shape—they are described as being set "on point" (fig C).

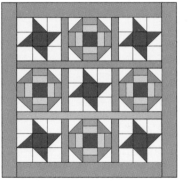

FIG B

FIG C

SPACER BLOCKS

Spacer blocks are secondary blocks set between more complicated block designs. They are often plain, so are perfect for quilting designs, but may be pieced in a simple way. They are used to set off the main blocks, to space them out visually, and to bring cohesion to a quilt if the decorated blocks all look very different. They are also a great way to stretch a small number of decorated blocks so there are enough to make up a quilt.

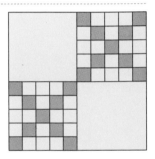

SQUARING UP BLOCKS

Before you begin joining blocks together, check that they are all the same size, right-angled and that they all have the same ¼" (6 mm) seam allowance. If some blocks are only slightly too large, you might be able to trim them down. Trim equally on each side so the design will still be centered.

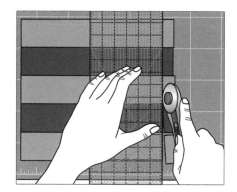

SASHING DESIGNS

"Sashing" refers to the strips of fabric used to separate blocks within a quilt top. Not all quilts have it, but it can be a good way to unite a design if the blocks used have clashing colors, or if they are very disparate designs.

Note

If the quilt is to be used on a bed, you may need to consider which blocks will come across the top and which will hang down at the sides and the end. With some block designs, the orientation will not matter, but others may need to be orientated so you view them the correct way up when the quilt is on the bed.

Note

If you can't adjust the size of a block easily, there is no alternative but to remake it, taking greater care, so that all the seam allowances are correct. When blocks are much too small, you could add a border all around to bring them up to the right size. If the block design is asymmetrical, try adding a border to only one or two sides.

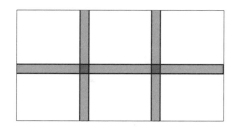

PLAIN TRELLIS WITH THE BLOCKS SET SQUARE
The sashing in one direction runs right across the quilt unbroken; in the other direction, the lines intersect. The unbroken lines of sashing can either run down the quilt or across it.

DIAGONAL TRELLIS
You can also set the trellis on the diagonal for blocks that are set on point. The lines of sashing can either intersect or have cornerstones.

PLAIN TRELLIS WITH CORNERSTONES
An alternative way of handling the point where the sashing lines intersect is to put in a corner square or cornerstone. This can be in the same or a contrasting fabric.

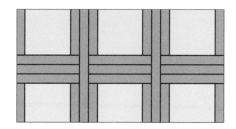

FRAMED BLOCKS WITH PLAIN TRELLIS
Individual blocks can be framed before they are sashed. Again, the sashing can intersect or have cornerstones.

JOINING BLOCKS WITHOUT SASHING

After individual blocks have been made and pressed, they all need to be joined together in some way. There are various standard ways to do this, but an almost endless variety of designs can be created. When joining blocks directly to each other, start by joining all the blocks into strips—you can either work in columns down the quilt (see below top), or in rows across (below bottom). Then join up the strips to make the finished quilt. Before you begin, plan your setting pattern (see page 140). It's a good idea to lay out all the blocks on a flat surface and stand back to judge the overall effect before you begin sewing.

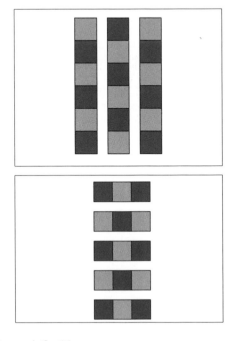

Some patchwork blocks work best when set directly alongside each other, without sashing strips to interrupt the pattern, as can be seen in the snail's trail quilt (pages 61–65).

JOINING BLOCKS WITH SASHING

Plan the sashing layout before you begin, trying out the blocks in different combinations to achieve the best effect. There are several ways to lay out sashing, so you can choose the one that best fits in with the design of your blocks (see Sashing Designs, page 141). The simplest way to add sashing is to incorporate sections of it between the appropriate blocks as you work. Plan your order of work before you begin.

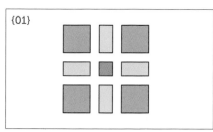

{01}

Decide on the width of the sashing and then add a ¼" (6 mm) seam allowance to both sides. Measure the length between a pair of blocks and cut the sashing to this length. Decide whether you want cornerstones. If so, these need to be square, and the same length as the width of the sashing strips, including seam allowances.

{02}

For an unbroken strip of sashing, work out the length required by measuring the finished block size (without seam allowances) and multiplying this by the number of blocks needed. Then measure the finished width of the intersecting sashing strip (without seam allowances), and multiply this by the number of intersecting sashing strips required between blocks. Add these measurements together, then add a ¼" (6 mm) seam allowance at each end.

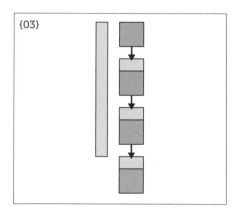

{03}

To join the sashing, first add an intersecting sashing strip to the top side of each block.

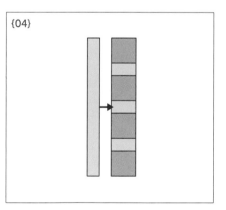

{04}

Join the blocks into a row, then add the continuous strip of sashing down one side of the row.

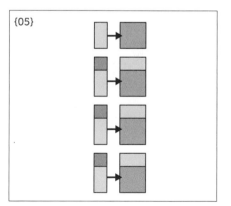

{05}

If you are using cornerstones, follow step 3. Then add a cornerstone to one end of each remaining strip of sashing. Stitch this strip of sashing, plus cornerstone, to one side of each block. Join the blocks in a row.

ADDING A BORDER

The final touch for the top of a quilt is often to add a border, but this is optional. The border can be plain or pieced and can be undecorated or have a quilted, embroidered or appliquéd design. You can also have multiple borders in toning or contrasting fabrics. The border should be a little wider than any sashing, for visual balance.

STRAIGHT BORDER

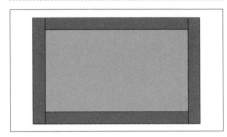

The simplest border is a straight border, made of a strip of fabric on each side of the quilt. Add the first two strips on opposite sides of the quilt first, then the two strips at either end. Usually, the shortest ends run across the longer (as shown here), but sometimes the longer sides run across the shorter.

CONTINUOUS BORDER

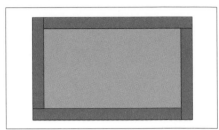

A continuous border runs around the quilt, overlapping at the ends in sequence. Cut the borders the length of the side, plus the width of the border. Apply the first strip at one side, leaving the extra length protruding at one end. Work around the quilt, adding each new strip across the end of the previous one. When you get back to the beginning, continue the stitching on the line of the first seam to catch the end of the last strip.

MITERED BORDER

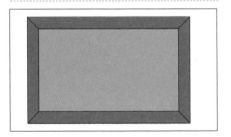

With a mitered corner, the two borders meet at the corner at a 45° angle and the angle must be precise. There are several ways to make a mitered border, but this method is one of the easiest. First, cut each border the length of the side plus two border widths.

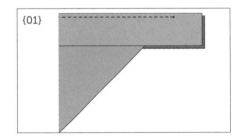

{01}

Center and stitch a border to each side, starting and finishing ¼" (5 mm) from the end. Press the borders flat, with the seams toward the border and the excess border at the corners overlapping. Fold the quilt at 45° through one corner, with right sides together and aligning the edges of excess border sections.

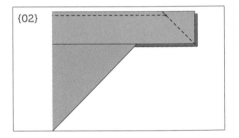

{02}

Beginning at the point where the side lines of stitching end, stitch across the border at 45°, in line with the diagonal made by the folded edge of the quilt. Trim away excess fabric, open out the quilt and press the mitered seam open.

CORNERSTONES

Cornerstones (also known as corner squares) cut from a contrasting fabric, add an extra feature to a quilt top.

Note

You could also add a pieced border, planning the design carefully so that all four corners match. If repeating units in the border and the quilt itself do not relate to each other, you can add a plain inner border between the two. Patchwork piecing that works well for borders are squares, four-patch rectangles, Seminole chevrons (pages 110–111) and flying geese (page 123).

Note

When choosing what type of border to have, consider the design of the quilt itself—the border should complement or add to the overall design, not overshadow it. If the quilt top is very complex, it may be better to opt for a plain border. The width of the border needs to be in scale with the rest of the design—if it is too narrow it may look skimpy, and if it is too wide it could look clumsy. If you need a very wide edging, think about having both an inner and an outer border.

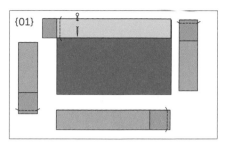

{01}

Cut the cornerstones with their sides the same measurement as the width of the border strip. Stitch a cornerstone to one end of each strip. Press seams to one side. Place the first strip along the edge of the quilt, right sides together, with the cornerstone overhanging the end. Begin stitching 4" (10 cm) from the cornerstone and continue to the end of the border.

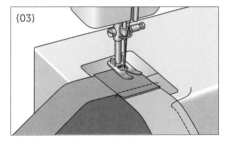

{03}

At the end, stitch the last border strip to the overhanging cornerstone and complete the first seam you made.

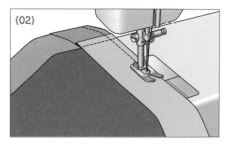

{02}

Place the next border strip with the cornerstone at the end of the border just sewn. Stitch the seam, then carry on adding the remaining border strips in the same way, working around the quilt clockwise.

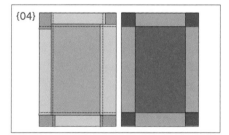

{04}

Press the seams to one side—in some places the construction of the border will dictate which way the seams can be pressed. On the front of the quilt, the border will have perfect contrast squares in each corner.

MAKING A QUILT SANDWICH

When the quilt top is finished it needs to be layered with backing fabric and batting in what is called a quilt sandwich. The batting forms the middle layer—without it the quilt is not technically a quilt. For information on the different types of batting and what they are used for, see page 89. The backing is the bottom layer of the quilt sandwich and generally should be the same weight and composition as the majority of the fabrics in the quilt top.

Note

To press a large quilt, try laying it out on a thick blanket on the floor or on a large table, or on a clean sheet over the mattress of a double bed. There are extra-large ironing boards available for quilters, which may be worth investing in if you plan to make a lot of patchwork quilts.

A bright orange fleece makes a colorful and comfortable backing for the hexagon picnic blanket (pages 30–33).

PREPARING THE BACKING

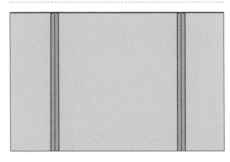

If the quilt top fabrics have been pre-shrunk, pre-shrink the backing too. Trim off the selvage and press well. Always cut the backing at least 2–4" (5–10 cm) bigger all round than the quilt top. You may need to join more than one length of fabric to make up the backing. Pay attention to where the seams fall, avoiding a seam falling in the middle of the quilt. Plan out the piecing of the backing—you may use less fabric if you place the seams horizontally rather than vertically. When the backing is ready lay it out right side down.

PREPARING THE BATTING

Use light-colored batting with light fabrics, and dark batting with dark fabrics. Batting is available in a range of weights, from light to heavy, so choose a suitable type depending on the use of the final quilt. Cut the batting at least 2–4" (5–10 cm) bigger all round than the quilt top, to allow for any pull during quilting. Lay it out flat overnight before use to allow any creases to drop out. Lay the batting on top of the backing and then lay the pressed quilt top on top, right side up, making sure you can see the batting and backing all around the edges.

SECURING THE QUILT SANDWICH

The layers of the quilt sandwich need to be held together ready for quilting. There are various ways to do this, from temporarily stitching (basting) or spray gluing the layers together, to bagging, where the quilt is turned inside out like a big pillowcase.

BASTING THE LAYERS

This can be done with rows of large running stitches or rows of safety pins. A special spray adhesive can also be used (see right). A bagged quilt should be basted after the bagging (see below) has been completed.

To minimize the layers shifting, begin basting or pinning in the center of the quilt, working out to the edges, spacing horizontal and vertical rows about 4" (10 cm) apart.

SPRAY GLUING THE LAYERS

Spray-on adhesive, which washes out, is also available to hold the quilt layers together ready for quilting. Make sure you follow the manufacturer's instructions and work in a well-ventilated area.

Lay the batting on a flat surface and spray lightly all over with temporary basting spray. Lay the backing fabric on top, right side up, and smooth it over the area carefully. Turn the whole thing over and spray the other side of the batting. Layer and smooth the quilt top fabric over the batting, right side up. The fabric layers are now ready for quilting.

BAGGING

Bagging is the process of joining the layers of the quilt together around the outside edges with right sides together, then turning the quilt right side out. This means the edges are finished and there is no need for binding. Quilting is done after bagging.

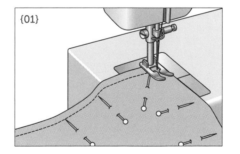

{01}

Lay the batting out flat with the quilt top, right side up, on top of it. Place the backing fabric on this, right side down. Smooth out wrinkles and pin or baste the layers together. Pin and then stitch around the outside edges, pivoting at the corners. Leave a gap 6–12" (15–30 cm) in one side, depending on the finished quilt size.

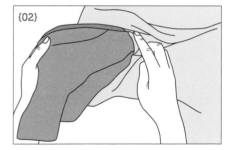

{02}

Trim seams and snip across corners close to the stitching. Turn the quilt right side out through the gap. Turn the raw edges under and slip stitch the gap to close.

QUILTING

When the layers of your quilt have been secured together you can move on to the quilting—some ideas are described here to get you started. These techniques are all suitable for a beginner and several have been used for the featured projects.

SIMPLE TIED QUILTING

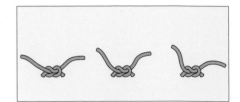

The advantage of tied quilting is that a very large area can be worked in the minimum amount of time. It also allows the batting to retain maximum loft, so it is great for use with heavyweight batting to create a really puffy quilt.

Quilt ties are often made in thick thread, but you can also use sturdy embroidery floss. Thread a needle and take it through the quilt top to the back, then back up again near the entry point. Tie the ends in a reef (square) knot: right over left, then left over right. You can also take a double stitch before knotting the ends, which can make the tie more secure.

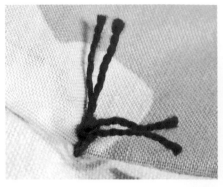

The layers of the giant rainbow star quilt (pages 14–19) are held together with simple ties worked in red embroidery floss.

HAND QUILTING

Hand quilting needs very little equipment, just a needle, thread and thimble, but it does take practice. With hand quilting the evenness of the stitches is more important than the length.

{01} Begin by tying a small knot in the end of your thread. Bring the needle and thread up from the back of the quilt to the front and pull gently on the thread until the knot pops through into the batting.

{02} Start quilting, pushing the needle down through the layers until you can feel it with your index finger. Rock the eye of the needle down toward the fabric and bring the tip of the needle to the surface a stitch length away. Rock the needle again to push it down through the fabric again. Repeat until you have several stitches loaded on to the needle and then pull the thread through. Repeat this process, following your marked design. To go from one area to be quilted to another you can feed the needle and thread through the batting.

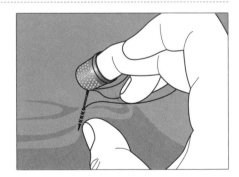

{03} To finish hand quilting tie a knot in the thread close to the quilt, put the needle through into the batting for a short distance and pop the knot into the batting. Trim off the thread.

MACHINE QUILTING

For speed, nothing beats machine quilting, yet the results can be very varied. A few key techniques are described here.

IN-THE-DITCH

This is quilting within the seam lines of a pieced pattern, or exactly around an appliqué outline. There is no need to mark the pattern. Use thread to tone with your fabrics, so the quilting is nearly invisible.

STRAIGHT LINES

To quilt in straight lines, either mark the full design on the quilt top, or just mark the first line and then use the foot as a guide to space the following lines an equal distance away. If the lines are spaced more widely apart, use a special bar (a quilting guide) that fits on the sewing machine to measure out the distance.

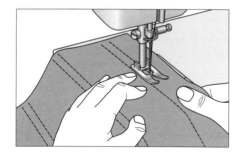

The layers of the Dresden plate tea cozy (pages 26–29) are machine quilted with a simple grid pattern.

Note

A standard machine will generally not have a large sewing area, so to make a big quilt more manageable, roll up the edges around the area you are working on and secure the rolls with quilt clips (or bicycle clips). A small table next to the machine table will also help support a large quilt.

OUTLINE AND ECHO

Outline quilting is similar to in-the-ditch quilting, but is positioned about ¼" (6 mm) away from the seam line, appliqué edges or motif. It can be worked inside or outside the line, or both. There is often no need to mark a pattern. With echo quilting, keep repeating the shape of the outline in lines of stitching at close intervals, radiating outward to fill the background.

CURVED LINES

Concentric curved lines are effective and can be marked out, or you can stitch the first one and then follow it with a quilting guide to space the next and following lines.

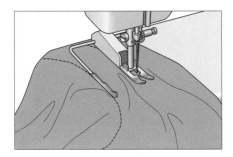

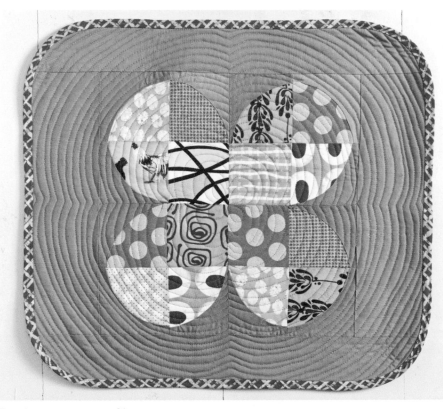

The placemats on page 81 were echo quilted, starting from the center and working outward, roughly following the floral motif of the piecing.

Note

When all quilting is finished, take all thread ends through to the back of the quilt, tie off in pairs and use a hand-sewing needle to bury the thread ends in the batting.

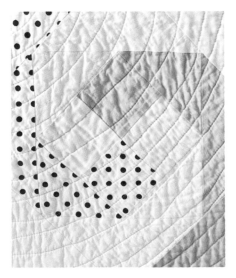

For the snail's trail quilt (page 62), a fairly free spiral pattern was quilted across the quilt.

BINDING

Unless it has been bagged, the raw edges of a quilt will need to be finished off using one of the techniques described in this section. Before binding, trim off excess batting and backing. Measure the quilt in three places across the width to check the measurements are the same. Do the same along the length, trimming if needed. Use a large rotary cutting mat to check that all corners are right angled.

JOINING BINDING STRIPS

When binding a large project such as a quilt, the likelihood is that you will need to join two or more strips of your chosen binding fabric.

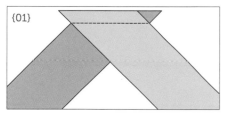

Pin the strips with right sides together—they will run at right angles to each other. Stitch together with a ³/₈" (1 cm) seam allowance.

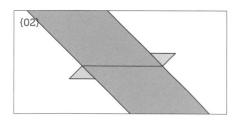

Press the seam open—remember that if the binding strip has a pattern you should try to match it on the seam line, not on the cut edges. Trim off the protruding points. If required, fold over a ¼" (6 mm) width of fabric to the wrong side along both edges.

SINGLE BINDING

Single binding uses less fabric than double binding, but will not protect the edges of the quilt so well, so it is best used for hangings. Usually quite narrow, it can be made in a color to contrast or tone with the quilt border.

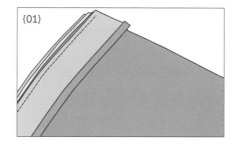

Cut four strips of binding the lengths of each side of the quilt and twice the width you want the binding to be, plus ³/₈" (1 cm) for seam allowances. Along one long edge of each strip, press a ¼" (6 mm) width of fabric to the wrong side. At each corner of the quilt, measure in ¼" (6 mm) from the edges and make a small mark. Place a binding strip down one edge of the quilt top, with right sides together and raw edges aligned—the folded edge of the binding should be toward the inner part of the quilt. Stitch in place between the corner marks only.

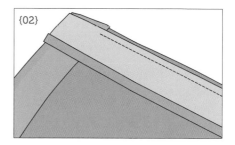

Fold the attached strip of binding up out of the way and pin a new strip along the next edge as before. Stitch between the marked corner points, again being careful not to catch the edge of the first strip as you begin sewing. Repeat for the remaining two strips.

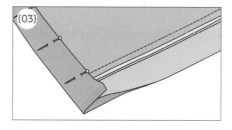

Fold the binding over to the back of the quilt, concealing the raw edges. Pin in place along the length of the side.

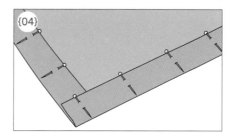

At the end of each strip, fold in the raw edges and square the corners. Pin in place and then slip stitch the binding to the backing along the fold line made in step 1, and at each corner.

CONTINUOUS BINDING

If you want to bind the edges of the quilt with a continuous strip of binding, you will probably need to join several strips to get the full length—see Joining Binding Strips, page 151. Measure the quilt around all four sides and prepare binding to this length, plus about 10" (25 cm) for seams and mitering at corners. Continuous binding can be single or double binding—just cut the strip to the appropriate width, usually 1½" (4 cm) for single-fold and 2½" (6.5cm) for double-fold. The diagrams here

Note

Binding can be very narrow or quite wide, in either a plain or a patterned fabric. You can use one of the fabrics already in the quilt or something totally new. It's usually best to choose the binding fabric when the quilt is finished, as it can be difficult to judge the effect before this. Spread out the quilt and try quite long strips of different lengths of fabric along the edge to see how they might look. Try out several options before making a final decision. Note: Your binding strips need only be cut on the bias if they have to be sewn around curved shapes.

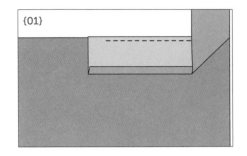

Beginning in the center of one side, place the binding strip along one edge of the quilt top, with right sides together and raw edges aligned—the folded edge of the binding should be facing toward the inner part of the quilt. Stitch to within ¼" (6 mm) of the edge of the quilt, then backstitch to secure. Remove the quilt from the machine. Fold the binding upward so a diagonal fold is formed and finger-press in place.

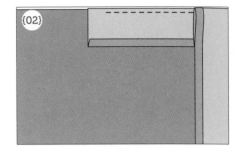

Now fold the binding strip down to align it with the next edge to be worked, holding the diagonal fold made in step 1 in place with your finger or a pin. Begin stitching down the new edge, starting at the top folded edge of the binding. Repeat at all four corners.

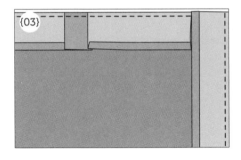

When you reach your starting position, fold the last ⅜" (1 cm) of the binding over and slide it under the raw edge of the first section of binding.

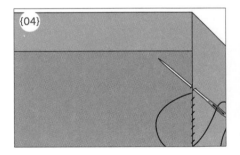

Turn the binding to the back of the quilt, and slip stitch the folded edge to the backing fabric as before. At each corner, fold the binding into a neat miter and slip stitch in place by hand.

TEMPLATES

Note: All templates to be used actual size unless otherwise specified.

Note: Copy the templates to the size you need, adding a ¼" (6 mm) seam allowance all around.

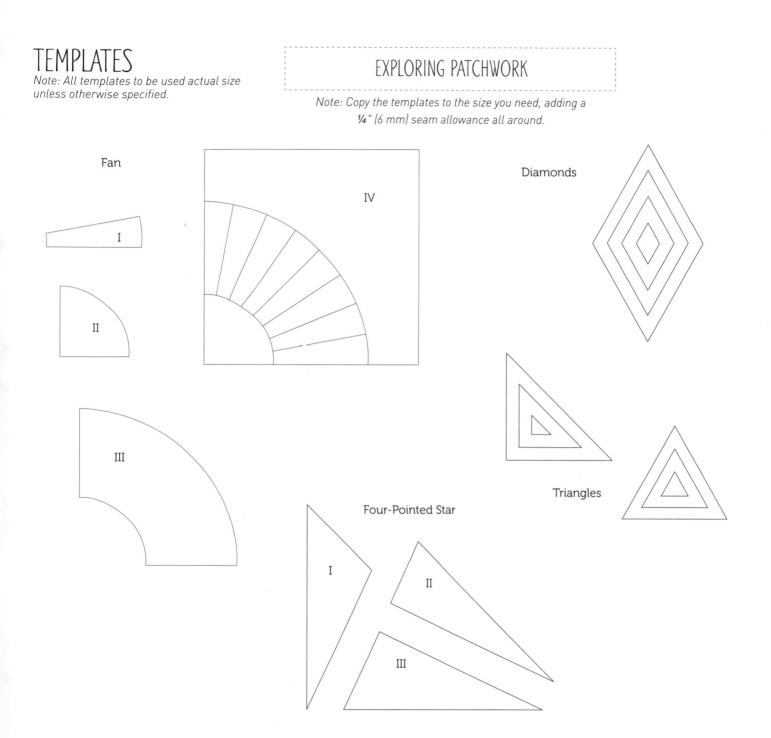

Fan

IV

Diamonds

III

Four-Pointed Star

Triangles

NINE-PATCH BEANBAG

Note: Enlarge by 200%.

Beetle appliqués

CLAMSHELL IPAD SLEEVE

Clamshell

RAIL FENCE OWL HANGING

Note: Enlarge by 200% and join along dashed lines.

Owl appliqué

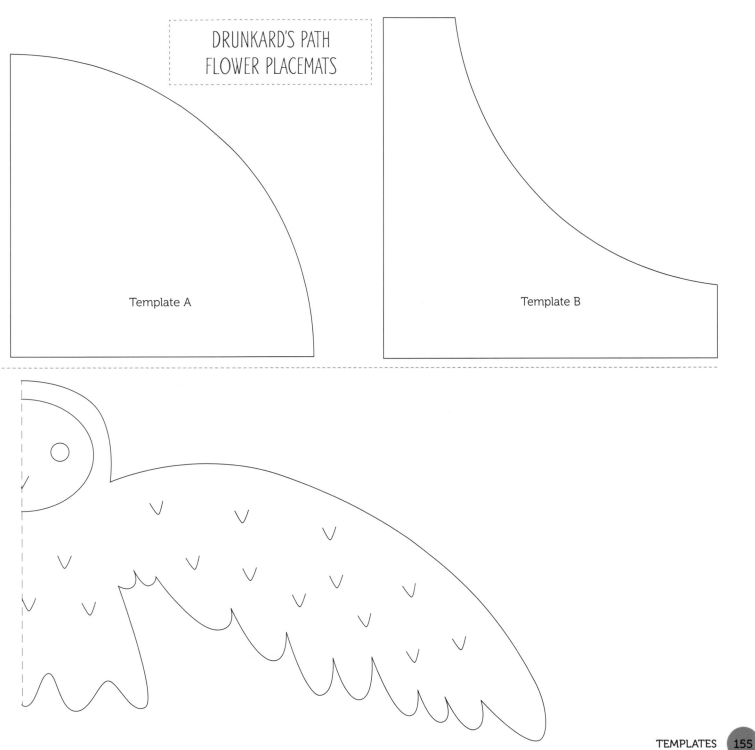

DRUNKARD'S PATH
FLOWER PLACEMATS

Template A

Template B

FOUNDATION-PIECED LAUNDRY BAG

Note: Enlarge the skirt, dress and bra paper piecing patterns by 200%.

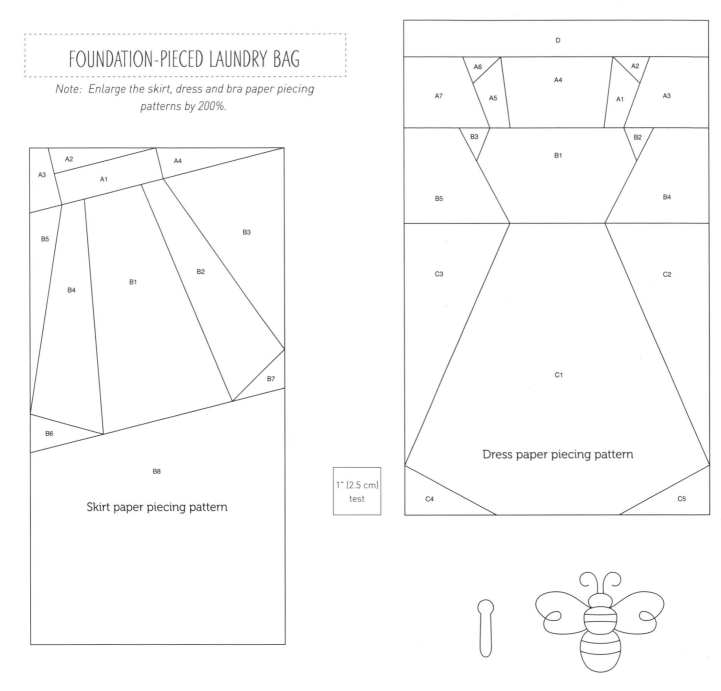

Skirt paper piecing pattern

1" (2.5 cm) test

Dress paper piecing pattern

Clothespin and bee embroidery motifs
Note: Actual size.

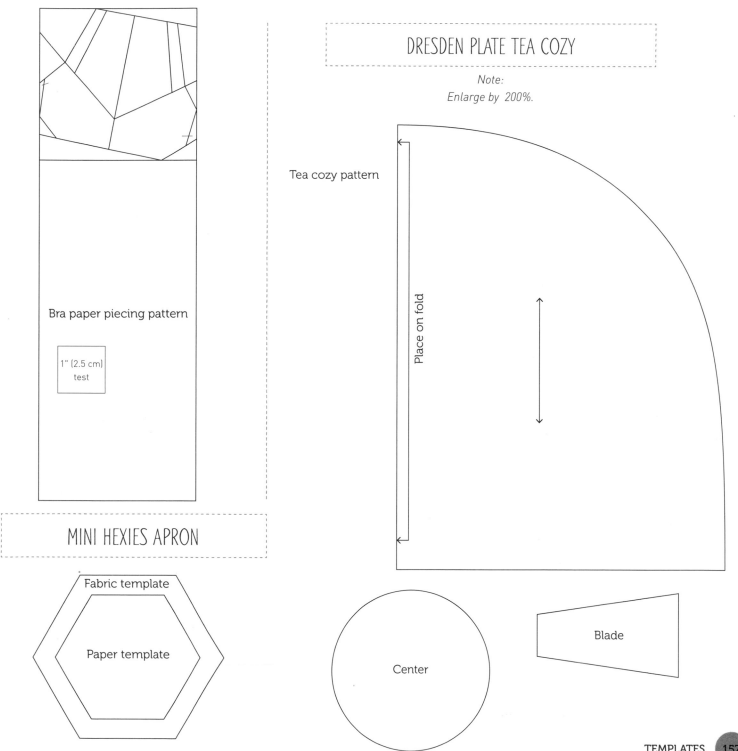

Bra paper piecing pattern

1" (2.5 cm)
test

Fabric template

Paper template

DRESDEN PLATE TEA COZY

Note:
Enlarge by 200%.

Tea cozy pattern

Place on fold

Center

Blade

HEXAGON PICNIC BLANKET

Note: Enlarge by 150%.

Print 2 and stick together on center line

Center line

INDEX

DIP INTO MORE *MOLLIE MAKES* INSPIRATION WITH THESE TITLES FROM INTERWEAVE

MOLLIE MAKES EMBROIDERY
Adorable Stitched Projects Plus Tips & Tricks
ISBN 978-1-59668-542-0 | $19.99

MOLLIE MAKES CROCHET
20+ Cute Projects for the Home Plus Handy Tips and Tricks
ISBN 978-1-62033-095-1 | $19.95

MOLLIE MAKES WEDDINGS
Projects & Ideas as Unique as You Are
ISBN 978-1-62033-541-3 | $12.99

PUBLISHER'S ACKNOWLEDGMENTS

This book would not have been possible without the input of our crafty contributors, who have provided all our brilliant how-to projects and step-by-step photography. We would also like to thank Cheryl Brown, who has done an excellent job of pulling everything together, and Sophie Martin for her design layout. Thanks to Mollie Johanson for allowing us to use her stitch diagrams. Main project photography by Rachel Whiting.

And of course, thanks must go to the fantastic team at *Mollie Makes* for all their help, in particular Lara Watson, Helena Tracey, Jane Toft, and Katherine Raderecht.

For more information on *Mollie Makes*, please visit molliemakes.com

First published in the United States in 2014 by

Interweave
A division of F+W, A Content
+ eCommerce Company
4868 Innovation Drive
Fort Collins, CO 80525
interweave.com

© 2014 Collins & Brown

ISBN 978-1-62033-543-7

Library of Congress Cataloging-in-Publication Data not available at time of printing.

10 9 8 7 6 5 4 3 2 1

Manufactured in China by 1010.